Martin Price

Lexcel Assessment Guide

Version 6 edition

Related titles from Law Society Publishing:

COFAs Toolkit
Jeremy Black and Florence Perret du Cray

COLPs Toolkit
Michelle Garlick

Conveyancing Protocol
The Law Society

In-house Lawyers' Toolkit
Richard Tapp and Ann Page

SRA Handbook (October 2014 edition)
Solicitors Regulation Authority

Wills and Inheritance Protocol
The Law Society

All books from Law Society Publishing can be ordered through good bookshops or direct from our distributors, Prolog, by telephone 0370 850 1422 or e-mail **lawsociety@prolog.uk.com**. Please confirm the price before ordering.

For further information or a catalogue, please contact our editorial and marketing office by e-mail **publishing@lawsociety.org.uk**.

Lexcel Assessment Guide

Version 6 edition

The Law Society

The Law Society

ISBN 978-1-78446-026-6

Published in 2015 by the Law Society
113 Chancery Lane, London WC2A 1PL

Typeset by Columns Design XML Ltd, Reading
Printed by Hobbs the Printers Ltd, Totton, Hants

The paper used for the text pages of this book is FSC® certified. FSC (the Forest Stewardship Council®) is an international network to promote responsible management of the world's forests.

FSC
www.fsc.org
MIX
Paper from responsible sources
FSC® C020438

Contents

Foreword

Practice management excellence is a crucial element for any effective law firm or in-house legal department. Practitioners should be committed to the promotion of service excellence in every aspect of their professional life. By doing so, society, practices and the profession can all benefit through the achievement of best practice.

Lexcel, the Law Society's legal practice quality mark, is aimed not only at providing a goal for practices to aspire to, but as an aid in developing management techniques. Legal practices – accredited or not – are utilising Lexcel's framework approach to achieve greater cost efficiencies, reductions in risks and client service excellence.

Lexcel can also help practitioners fulfil their obligations in an increasingly complex regulatory environment. This continuing pressure is eased with accreditation, as the structure promoted within Lexcel ensures that solicitors analyse their business operations on a regular basis. This can, in particular, help a practice and in-house legal departments to comply with the SRA Code of Conduct 2011.

Practices can use the Lexcel Standard to demonstrate a framework which facilitates compliance with multiple requirements within the Code. The Standard does go further, however, requiring policies and procedures to enhance practice beyond what is asked for in certain areas of the Code. Risk management is an area that continues to be an ever-developing concern for solicitors. In this case, the Lexcel framework can improve the identification and implementation of preventative action quickly to minimise risks to the practice and its clients.

Lexcel can help any practice, regardless of size or type of work undertaken. Sole practitioners to large private practices and legal departments alike can all benefit. The flexibility the Standard offers can suit a wide range of practices develop management techniques that help manage risk and enhance service. I thoroughly recommend it to you.

Andrew Caplen
President (2014–15)
The Law Society

Preface

With ever-increasing competitive forces and client demands, it is vital to manage the quality and delivery of legal services. A quality management system demonstrates commitment and an ability to consistently deliver services that meet client expectations, improve overall satisfaction and assist with regulatory compliance.

Designed specifically for the legal sector, Lexcel is the Law Society's Standard for excellence in practice management and client care. It provides a flexible and supportive management framework to enable practices to operate more efficiently, improve client care, manage risk effectively, reduce costs and promote profitability.

Lexcel defines quality management procedures in seven areas: structure and strategy, financial management, information management, people management, risk management, client care and file and case management. There are separate standards for legal practices and in-house legal departments.

Practices and departments are required to achieve and maintain the requirements set out in the Standard. How such requirements are met is for individual practices and departments to decide, based on their specific needs and circumstances. Most practices and departments will document all of their policies and procedures in an office manual; however, the required information may be set out in a variety of sources.

An independent assessment process ensures that the requirements of the Standard have been met. This publication is a guide to each requirement of the Standard for practices and departments. It provides examples of the evidence an assessor will require to validate that the Standard has been met.

The requirements of the Standard for both practices and departments are on the whole mandatory in nature and these are indicated by the use of the word 'must'. There are some optional requirements which may not always be appropriate to all practices and departments and these are indicated by the use of the word 'should'. A glossary of terms can be found at the beginning of each Standard.

If, after reading this assessment guide, you have any questions regarding Lexcel, please do not hesitate to contact us on:

Tel: +44 (0)20 7320 5933
E-mail: lexcel@lawsociety.org.uk

The Lexcel office would like to thank Kamran Hussain and Chantal Ben-Nathan for their work in creating this assessment guide.

March 2015

PART I

The Standard for legal practices

Introduction

WHO IS LEXCEL FOR?

- Legal practices in any jurisdiction in the world can apply for accreditation against the Lexcel Standard, regardless of the size or type of work undertaken. See the **Scheme rules** for further details.
- Two versions of Lexcel are available to reflect the needs of domestic and international markets:
  - **Lexcel England and Wales** – version 6 of the Standard for legal practices in England and Wales.
  - **Lexcel International** – version 5 of the Standard for practices in England and Wales with independent offices overseas and practices in foreign jurisdictions.
- Lexcel England and Wales is divided into two versions to meet the needs of legal practices and in-house legal departments. These entities are defined as:
  - **A law practice** in the form of partnerships, limited liability partnerships, sole practitioners, incorporated law firms and alternative business structures (ABSs) authorised and regulated by the Solicitors Regulation Authority (SRA).
  - **An in-house legal department,** including those in corporations, the public sector (including ABSs), law centres, not-for-profit and government organisations.
- For ease of reference, the generic term 'practice' is used throughout the Standard.
- Practices whose head office is in England and Wales must be authorised and regulated by the SRA.
- Practices with multiple offices can apply by jurisdiction. For example, a law firm with five offices across England and Wales must submit one application and be assessed across all five offices. In contrast, one that has two offices in England and Wales and an independent office overseas would need to submit two applications, if they wanted to apply for Lexcel across multiple jurisdictions. It is not mandatory for all offices across multiple jurisdictions to apply for Lexcel. Please see the **Scheme rules** for further details.
- Lexcel can be combined with other quality standards including ISO 9001, Investors in People and the Specialist Quality Mark (SQM) and could reduce the time and cost of assessment. A joint assessment may also be possible.
- Lexcel is accepted as a quality standard by the Legal Aid Agency, instead of accreditation against the SQM.
- An annual practice registration fee is payable to the Law Society and a fee is also payable to the independent assessment body.
- The annual practice registration fee is divided into five bands, based on the total number of admitted and non-admitted fee earners at the practice:

- 1 fee earner
- 2 – 15 fee earners
- 16 – 40 fee earners
- 41 – 85 fee earners
- 86+ fee earners

GLOSSARY OF TERMS AND GUIDANCE

- **Emphasised words** in the Lexcel Standard are defined in the **Glossary of Terms.**
- A main requirement is presented as a numbered paragraph. Specific requirements are listed as subclauses.
- Separate **Guidance notes** provide further explanation of requirements and are divided into general and specific guidance based on the practice size:
  - General guidance – All practices
  - Specific guidance – For practices with 1 fee earner
  - Specific guidance – For small and medium practices (2–85 fee earners)
  - Specific guidance – For large practices (86+ fee earners)
- Practices have the flexibility to implement procedures that are appropriate to their circumstances in order to meet requirements in the Standard.
- Most practices will document all procedures in an office manual, but there is no specific requirement that prevents procedures being documented in a number of different sources.
- Although Lexcel will help practices comply with some aspects of legislation, accreditation does not guarantee compliance with local laws. This remains the responsibility of the practice.

The Lexcel Standard for legal practices

GLOSSARY OF TERMS

Term	Definition
Authorisations	Practices need to consider whether authorisation **procedures** need to be in place whereby different **personnel** are given permission to approve expenditure to pre-defined levels.
Corporate social responsibility (CSR)	For the purposes of Lexcel, **CSR** is defined as the commitment by a practice to operate in an ethical manner and contribute in a positive way to society. This is an optional requirement for practices, although practices tendering for the provision of legal services to organisations may be required to have a **CSR policy** in place.
Evaluation	To make a judgement.
Flexible working	**Flexible working** practices have become increasingly relevant to the legal sector as part of recruitment and retention. Some examples of **flexible working** are part time working, annualised hours, compressed hours and remote working.
Malicious software (malware)	Software that is used to disrupt computer operation, gather sensitive data or gain access to private computer systems.
Must	A mandatory requirement.
Objectives	Any **objectives** agreed and set out need to be measurable. They will require some form of quantification or have indicators of progress to measure performance.
Personnel	All employed staff which includes a principal, locums, partners, members and directors.
Plan(s)	A **'plan'** is a documented outline of where a practice desires to be in the future and describes how it intends to arrive at that destination. A **plan** can be described as a map which supports practices to arrive at their desired destination in the future. In general, the Lexcel Standard permits practices to develop **plans** in the manner and detail that the practice considers appropriate, assuming a basic level of adequacy. All **plans must** have a named person who is responsible for the **plan**. They **must** also be reviewed at least annually.
Policy/policies	A **'policy'** is a documented general approach taken within the practice to the issue in question. A **policy** defines why a particular approach is adopted by the practice. All **policies must** have a named person who is responsible for the **policy**. They **must** also be reviewed at least annually.
Procedure(s)	A **'procedure'** is a written description of how an activity will occur within the practice. A **procedure** describes the steps that **personnel** are required to follow in order to complete an activity. At an assessment, a **procedure** can only be said to be complied with if the assessor can observe that the **procedure** contained in the practice's documentation is in effective operation. All **procedures must** have a named person who is responsible for the **procedure**. They **must** also be reviewed at least annually.

Reasonable adjustments	The duty to make **reasonable adjustments** is a legal responsibility under anti-discrimination legislation. The requirement is intended to make sure that disabled people do not face difficulties in employment, education or when using services. A **reasonable adjustment** is a reasonable step taken to prevent a disabled person suffering a substantial disadvantage compared with people who are not disabled.
Register	Multiple records that are held in hard copy or electronic format.
Risk register	A **risk register** is a record of the risks facing the practice. There is no fixed format for the **risk register** prescribed by Lexcel. It should indicate who has responsibility for a particular risk and any measures taken by the practice to mitigate or reduce the risk.
Role profile	A description of the role undertaken by an individual including the key purpose of the role, summary of responsibilities and the skills and experience required of the individual.
Should	An optional requirement. In some cases, practices may be required to explain why they have chosen not to implement a requirement by their Lexcel assessor.
Strategic plan	A strategic plan identifies the practice's goals and the activities necessary to achieve those goals.
Supervisor(s)	A person(s) who is(are) of sufficient seniority and in a position of sufficient responsibility with the appropriate skills and experience to guide and assist others.

1 STRUCTURE AND STRATEGY

1.1 Practices *must* have documentation setting out the:

(a) legal framework under which they operate
(b) management structure which designates the responsibilities of individuals and their accountability.

1.2 Practices *must* have a strategic *plan*, which *must* include:

(a) *objectives* for at least the next 12 months
(b) the identification of resources required to meet the *objectives*
(c) the services the practice wishes to offer
(d) the client groups to be served
(e) how services will be delivered and marketed
(f) a documented risk *evaluation* of *objectives*
(g) *procedures* for regular reporting on performance.

1.3 Practices *must* have a business continuity *plan*, which *must* include:

(a) an *evaluation* of potential risks that could lead to business interruption
(b) ways to reduce, avoid and/or transfer the risks
(c) key people relevant to the implementation of the *plan*
(d) a *procedure* to test the *plan* annually, to verify that it would be effective in the event of a business interruption.

1.4 Practices *should* have a *policy* in relation to *corporate social responsibility*.

2 FINANCIAL MANAGEMENT

2.1 Practices *must* document the person who has overall responsibility for financial management.

2.2 Practices *must* be able to provide documentary evidence of their financial management *procedure*, including:

(a) annual budget including income and expenditure
(b) annual income and expenditure accounts
(c) annual balance sheet
(d) annual income and expenditure forecast to be reviewed quarterly
(e) variance analysis conducted at least quarterly of income and expenditure against budgets
(f) variance analysis conducted at least quarterly of cash flow and cash flow forecast.

2.3 Practices *should* have a time recording *procedure*.

2.4 Practices *must* have a *procedure* in relation to billing clients, which *must* include:

(a) the frequency and terms for billing clients
(b) credit limits for new and existing clients
(c) debt management.

2.5 Practices handling financial transactions *must* have a *procedure*, which *must* include:

(a) the transfer of funds
(b) the management of funds received by the practice
(c) *authorisations*.

3 INFORMATION MANAGEMENT

3.1 Practices *must* have an information management and security *policy*, which *must* include:

(a) a *register* of relevant information assets of both the practice and clients
(b) *procedures* for the protection and security of the information assets
(c) *procedures* for the retention and disposal of information
(d) the use of firewalls
(e) *procedures* for the secure configuration of network devices
(f) *procedures* to manage user accounts
(g) *procedures* to detect and remove *malicious software*
(h) a *register* of all software used by the practice
(i) training for *personnel* on information security
(j) a *plan* for the updating and monitoring of software.

3.2 Practices *must* have an e-mail *policy*, which *must* include:

(a) the scope of permitted and prohibited use
(b) *procedures* for monitoring *personnel* using e-mail
(c) *procedures* for the storage and destruction of e-mails.

3.3 If the practice has a website, the practice *must* have a website management *policy*, which *must* include:

(a) a *procedure* for content approval, publishing and removal
(b) the scope of permitted and prohibited content
(c) *procedures* for the management of its security
(d) consideration of accessibility requirements for disabled clients.

3.4 Practices *must* have an internet access *policy*, which *must* include:

(a) the scope of permitted and prohibited use
(b) *procedures* for monitoring *personnel* accessing the internet.

3.5 Practices *must* have a social media *policy*, which *must* include:

(a) a *procedure* for participating in social media on behalf of the practice
(b) the scope of permitted and prohibited content.

3.6 Practices *must* have:

(a) a *register* of each *plan*, *policy* and *procedure* that is contained in the Lexcel Standard
(b) a named person responsible for each *policy*, *plan* and *procedure* that is contained in the Lexcel Standard
(c) a *procedure* for the review of each *policy*, *plan* and *procedure* that is contained in the Lexcel Standard.

4 PEOPLE MANAGEMENT

4.1 Practices *must* have a *policy* in relation to the health and safety of all *personnel* and visitors to the practice.

4.2 Practices *must* have an equality and diversity *policy*, which *must* include:

(a) recruitment, selection and progression
(b) a *procedure* to deal with complaints and disciplinary issues in breach of the *policy*
(c) a *procedure* to monitor diversity and collate equality data
(d) training of all *personnel* on compliance with equality and diversity requirements
(e) *procedures* for *reasonable adjustments* for *personnel*.

4.3 Practices *must* have a learning and development *policy*, which *must* include:

(a) ensuring that appropriate training is provided to *personnel* within the practice
(b) ensuring that all *supervisors* and managers receive appropriate training
(c) a *procedure* to evaluate training
(d) a learning and development *plan* for all *personnel*.

4.4 Practices *must* list the tasks to be undertaken by all *personnel* within the practice usually in the form of a *role profile*.

4.5 Practices *must* have *procedures* to deal effectively with recruitment selection and progression, which *must* include:

(a) the identification of vacancies
(b) the drafting of the job documentation
(c) methods of attracting candidates

(d) clear and transparent selection
(e) storage, retention and destruction of records
(f) references and ID checking
(g) where appropriate, the checking of disciplinary records.

4.6 Practices *must* conduct an appropriate induction for all *personnel*, including those transferring roles within the practice and *must* cover:

(a) the management structure and the individual's responsibilities
(b) terms and conditions of employment
(c) immediate training requirements
(d) key *policies*.

4.7 Practices *must* have a *procedure* which details the steps to be followed when a member of *personnel* ceases to be an employee, which *must* include:

(a) the handover of work
(b) exit interviews
(c) the return of property belonging to the practice.

4.8 Practices *must* have a performance management *policy*, which *must* include:

(a) the practice's approach to performance management
(b) performance review periods and timescales.

4.9 Practices *must* have a whistleblowing *policy*.
4.10 Practices *must* have a *flexible working policy*.

5 RISK MANAGEMENT

5.1 Practices *must* have a risk management *policy*, which *must* include:

(a) a compliance *plan*
(b) a *risk register*
(c) defined risk management roles and responsibilities
(d) arrangements for communicating risk information.

5.2 Practices *must* have a *policy* in relation to outsourced activities, which *must* include:

(a) details of all outsourced activities including providers
(b) *procedures* to check the quality of outsourced work
(c) *procedures* to ensure providers have taken appropriate precautions to ensure information will be protected.

5.3 There *must* be a named *supervisor* for each area of work undertaken by the practice.
5.4 Practices *must* have *procedures* to manage instructions, which may be undertaken even though they have a higher *risk profile*, including unusual supervisory and reporting requirements or contingency planning.
5.5 Practices *must* maintain lists of work that the practice will and will not undertake. This information *must* be communicated to all relevant *personnel* and *must* be updated when changes occur.

5.6 Practices *must* maintain details of the generic risks and causes of claims associated with the area(s) of work undertaken by the practice. This information *must* be communicated to all relevant *personnel*.

5.7 Practices *must* have a *procedure* to monitor key dates, which *must* include:

(a) the definition of key dates by work type
(b) ensuring that key dates are recorded on the file and in a back-up system.

5.8 Practices *must* have a *policy* on the handling of conflicts, which *must* include:

(a) the definition of conflicts
(b) training for all relevant *personnel* to identify conflicts
(c) steps to be followed when a conflict is identified.

5.9 Practices *must* have a *procedure* to ensure that all *personnel*, both permanent and temporary, are actively supervised. Such *procedures must* include:

(a) checks on incoming and outgoing correspondence where appropriate
(b) departmental, team and office meetings and communication structures
(c) reviews of matter details in order to ensure good financial controls and the appropriate allocation of workloads
(d) the exercise of devolved powers in publicly funded work
(e) the availability of a *supervisor*
(f) allocation of new work and reallocation of existing work, if necessary.

5.10 Practices *must* have a *procedure* to ensure that all those doing legal work check their files regularly for inactivity.

5.11 Practices *must* have a *procedure* for regular, independent file reviews of either the management of the file or its substantive legal content, or both. In relation to file reviews, practices *must*:

(a) define and explain file selection criteria
(b) define and explain the number and frequency of reviews
(c) retain a record of the file review on the matter file and centrally
(d) ensure any corrective action, which is identified in a file review, is acted upon within 28 days and verified
(e) ensure that the designated *supervisor* reviews and monitors the data generated by file reviews
(f) conduct a review at least annually of the data generated by file reviews.

5.12 Operational risk *must* be considered and recorded in all matters before, during and after the processing of instructions. Before the matter is undertaken, the fee earners *must*:

(a) consider if a new client and/or matter, is accepted by the practice, in accordance with section 6.1 and 6.7 below
(b) assess the risk profile of all new instructions and notify the *supervisor*, in accordance with *procedures* under 5.4, of any unusual or high risk considerations in order that appropriate action may be taken.

During the retainer the fee earner *must*:

(c) consider any change to the *risk profile* of the matter and report and advise on such circumstances without delay, informing the *supervisor* if appropriate
(d) inform the client in all cases where an adverse costs order is made against the practice in relation to the matter in question.

At the end of the matter the fee earner *must*:

- **(e) undertake a concluding risk assessment by considering if the client's *objectives* have been achieved**
- **(f) notify the *supervisor* of all such circumstances in accordance with documented *procedures* in section 5.4 above.**

5.13 Practices *must* have a *policy* to ensure compliance with anti-money laundering legislation, which *must* include:

- **(a) the appointment of a nominated officer usually referred to as a Money Laundering Reporting Officer (MLRO)**
- **(b) a *procedure* for making disclosures within the practice and by the MLRO to the authorities**
- **(c) *procedures* for checking the identity of the practice's clients**
- **(d) a *plan* for the training of *personnel***
- **(e) *procedures* for the proper maintenance of records.**

5.14 Practices *should* have a *policy* in relation to the avoidance of involvement in property and mortgage fraud, which *must* include:

- **(a) carrying out relevant checks in relation to the conveyancer acting for the other party.**

5.15 Practices *must* have a *policy* setting out the *procedures* to prevent bribery in accordance with current legislation.

5.16 Practices will analyse at least annually all risk assessment data generated within the practice. This *must* include:

- **(a) any indemnity insurance claims (where applicable)**
- **(b) an analysis of client complaints trends**
- **(c) data generated by file reviews**
- **(d) any matters notified to the COLP and/or COFA**
- **(e) any material breaches notified to the SRA**
- **(f) any non-material breaches recorded**
- **(g) situations where the practice acted where a conflict existed**
- **(h) the identification of remedial action.**

6 CLIENT CARE

6.1 Practices *must* have a *policy* for client care, including:

- **(a) how enquiries from potential clients will be dealt with**
- **(b) ensuring that before taking on a client, the practice has sufficient resources and competence to deal with the matter**
- **(c) protecting client confidentiality**
- **(d) a timely response is made to telephone calls and correspondence from the client and others**
- **(e) a *procedure* for referring clients to third parties**
- **(f) the provision of *reasonable adjustments* for disabled clients.**

6.2 Practices *must* communicate the following to clients in writing, unless an alternative form of communication is deemed more appropriate:

(a) where appropriate, establish the client's requirements and *objectives*
(b) provide a clear explanation of the issues involved and the options available to the client
(c) explain what the fee earner will and will not do
(d) agree with the client the next steps to be taken
(e) keep the client informed of progress, as agreed
(f) establish in what timescale that matter will be dealt with
(g) establish the method of funding
(h) where appropriate, consider whether the intended action would be merited on a cost benefit analysis
(i) agree an appropriate level of service
(j) explain the practice's responsibilities and the client's
(k) provide the client with the name and status of the person dealing with their matter
(l) provide the client with the name and status of the person responsible for the overall supervision of their matter.

6.3 Practices *must* have a record of any standing terms of business with regular clients. The practice *must* be able to produce such terms in relation to issues covered by this section.

6.4 Practices *must* give clients the best information possible about the likely overall cost of the matter, both at the outset and when appropriate, as the matter progresses. In particular practices *must*:

(a) advise the client of the basis of the practice's charging
(b) advise the client where the practice will receive a financial benefit as a result of accepting instructions
(c) advise the client if the charging rates are to be increased
(d) advise the client of likely payments which the practice or the client may need to make to others
(e) discuss with the client how they will pay
(f) advise the client that there are circumstances where the practice may be entitled to exercise a lien for unpaid costs
(g) advise the client of their potential liability for any other party's costs.

6.5 Practices *must* operate a written complaints handling *procedure*, including:

(a) the definition of what the practice regards as a complaint
(b) informing the client at the outset of the matter, that in the event of a problem they are entitled to complain
(c) the name of the person with overall responsibility for complaints
(d) providing the client with a copy of the practice's complaints *procedure*, if requested
(e) once a complaint has been made, the person complaining is informed in writing:

(i) how the complaint will be handled; and
(ii) in what time they will be given an initial and/or substantive response

(f) recording and reporting centrally all complaints received from clients
(g) identifying the cause of any problems of which the client has complained, offering any appropriate redress, and correcting any unsatisfactory *procedures*.

6.6 Practices *must* have a *procedure* to monitor client satisfaction across all areas of the practice.

6.7 Practices *must* have a *procedure* to accept or decline instructions, which *must* include:

(a) how decisions are made to accept instructions from new and existing clients
(b) how decisions are made to stop acting for an existing client
(c) how decisions are made to decline instructions.

7 FILE AND CASE MANAGEMENT

7.1 Practices *must* ensure that the strategy for a matter is always apparent on the matter file and that in complex cases a project plan is developed.

7.2 Practices *must* document *procedures* for the giving, monitoring and discharge of undertakings.

7.3 Practices *must* have a *procedure* to:

(a) list open and closed matters, identify all matters for a single client and linked files where relevant and all files for a particular funder
(b) ensure that they are able to identify and trace any documents, files, deeds, wills or any other items relating to the matter
(c) safeguard the confidentiality of matter files and all other client information
(d) ensure that the status of the matter and the action taken can be easily checked by other members of the practice
(e) ensure that documents are stored on the matter file(s) in an orderly way.

7.4 Practices will have *procedures* to ensure that matters are progressed in an appropriate manner. In particular:

(a) key information *must* be recorded on the file
(b) a timely response is made to telephone calls and correspondence from the client and others
(c) continuing cost information is provided
(d) clients are informed in writing if the person with conduct of their matter changes, or there is a change of person to whom any problem with service may be addressed.

7.5 Practices *must* have a documented *procedure* for using barristers, expert witnesses and other external advisers who are involved in the delivery of legal services, which *must* include provision for the following:

(a) use of clear selection criteria in line with the equality and diversity *policy*
(b) where appropriate, consult with the client in relation to the selection of an advocate or other professional
(c) advising the client of the name and status of the person being instructed, how long she/he might take to respond and, where disbursements are to be paid by the client, the cost involved
(d) maintenance of records (centrally, by department or office) on barristers and experts used, including evidence of assessment against the criteria
(e) *evaluation* of performance, for the information of other members of the practice
(f) giving clear instructions
(g) checking of opinions and reports received to ensure they adequately provide the information sought (and, in litigation matters, comply with the rules of court and any court orders)
(h) payment of fees.

7.6 Practices *must* have *procedures* to ensure that, at the end of the matter, the practice:

(a) if required, reports to the client on the outcome and explains any further action that the client is required to take in the matter and what (if anything) the practice will do
(b) accounts to the client for any outstanding money
(c) returns to the client any original documents or other property belonging to the client if required (save for items which are by agreement to be stored by the practice)
(d) if appropriate, advises the client about arrangements for storage and retrieval of papers and other items retained (in so far as this has not already been dealt with, for example in terms of business) and any charges to be made in this regard
(e) advises the client whether it is appropriate to review the matter in future and, if so, when and why
(f) archives and destroys files in an appropriate manner.

Assessment criteria

1 STRUCTURE AND STRATEGY

Section 1 deals with issues concerning the strategic direction of practices and the structure that is in place to assist practices to achieve their goals.

1.1 Practices *must* have documentation setting out the:

(a) legal framework under which they operate
(b) management structure which designates the responsibilities of individuals and their accountability.

There are a range of business structures that practices can adopt to deliver legal services. The most common structure for practices is a partnership. However, limited liability partnerships (LLPs), sole practitioners, incorporated law firms and alternative business structures (ABSs) regulated by the Solicitors Regulation Authority (SRA) are also valid business structures.

Practices that are partnerships must have a partnership agreement in place. The partnership agreement should deal with the following issues:

(a) management and voting rights;
(b) the authorisation of individual partners or managers to bind a practice in contract;
(c) rights to share in profits;
(d) how capital contributions will be dealt with and rights to interest;
(e) how capital will be repaid;
(f) entry to and expulsions and retirements from a practice;
(g) the rights of partners to elect part-time working patterns and provisions for parental leave, including maternity provisions;
(h) the effect of long-term illness or incapacity of the partners;
(i) how succession will be achieved; and
(j) continuity of a practice in the event of death or incapacity in the case of small and medium sized practices and sole practitioners.

The documents setting out the legal framework under which a practice operates may be highly sensitive and therefore it is permissible for practices to decline to disclose such documents to their assessor. Practices that choose not to disclose the documents should be able to discuss the broad themes included in the documentation to satisfy their assessor that they have complied with this requirement.

All practices should be able to provide their assessor with confirmation from the SRA that they are an authorised body. The form of evidence that needs to be provided can vary and may include producing a certificate of authorisation or referring to the Law Society's Find a Solicitor website.

The management structure which designates the responsibilities of individuals and their accountability may be presented as an organisational chart. Alternative formats are acceptable provided that they communicate the information required by 1.1(b).

Sole practitioners: Sole practitioners should be able to produce evidence of the legal framework under which they operate, for example a certificate of incorporation confirming that they are a limited company or confirmation from the SRA that they are an authorised body, usually in the form of an authorisation certificate.

It is not necessary to document the requirements set out in 1.1(b). However, sole practitioners should be able to discuss their responsibilities with their assessor.

Small and medium practices: Small and medium sized practices must be able to produce evidence of the legal framework under which they operate, for example a partnership agreement or a certificate of incorporation.

It is also possible to satisfy 1.1(a) by practices setting out details of their legal framework in their office manual.

Small and medium sized practices will be required to set out their management structure, including designated responsibilities and accountability. This information is often presented in an organisational chart or table. A combination of both may be useful for medium sized practices, where there is a greater volume of information to convey.

Practices may wish to set out together the information required in 1.1(b) and 3.6.

Large practices: Large practices must be able to produce evidence of the legal framework under which they operate, for example a partnership agreement or a certificate of incorporation. This documentation should include information relating to a practice's corporate governance. This would typically include the following:

- ownership structure;
- voting rights; and
- roles and responsibilities.

It is also possible to satisfy 1.1(a) by practices setting out details of their legal framework in their office manual or corporate governance documentation.

In order to meet the requirements in 1.1(b) large practices may wish to have a number of organisational charts which taken together cover the whole practice. It may be helpful to divide the organisational charts by department, work types, teams, offices or a combination of all of these.

It is possible to choose to name roles rather than individuals in the management structure as this will reduce the need to frequently update documentation as members of personnel change.

Assessment note: Practices are encouraged to provide their assessor with documentation to demonstrate the requirement at 1.1(a). In the event that a practice deems that the documentation setting out its legal framework is too sensitive to disclose, an assessor may accept interview evidence instead.

In relation to 1.1(b) a practice should be able to produce documentary evidence of the management structure which sets out the responsibilities of individuals and their accountability. In addition to having access to such documentation, assessors will gather interview evidence to confirm that the management structure and responsibilities within practices are understood.

1.2 Practices *must* have a strategic *plan*, which *must* include:

(a) *objectives* for at least the next 12 months
(b) the identification of resources required to meet the *objectives*
(c) the services the practice wishes to offer
(d) the client groups to be served
(e) how services will be delivered and marketed
(f) documented risk *evaluation* of *objectives*
(g) *procedures* for regular reporting on performance.

The strategic plan needs to set out a practice's overall direction. The format of the strategic plan is flexible and will need to reflect the culture of a practice. Typically, the strategic plan is an internal planning tool that is often the basis for a more detailed business plan. In some practices this may be achieved through a combination of different documents, for example a strategic plan for their practice together with a series of departmental plans. The factors that will determine the complexity of the strategic documentation will include:

- the size of a practice – sole practitioners and small practices will usually have simpler strategies and less need for complex documentation;
- whether much change is anticipated over the period of the plan – a practice seeking to consolidate or stabilise its current operations will probably have less to address than one that is expanding; and
- the management style of the partners or directors.

1.2(a) requires that objectives are set for the next 12 months. This is a minimum length of time and ideally the strategic plan should include objectives for the next three to five years. The objectives should be SMART (Specific, Measureable, Achievable, Realistic and Time-bound) to assist in establishing the level of progress made towards the objectives. If practices choose to have objectives for a longer period of time than required by this section, the objectives for the next 12 months should be more detailed than the medium- or long-term objectives.

The resources that practices need to consider in the context of 1.2(b) are:

- people (HR);
- finance;
- technology; and
- facilities.

It is important that practices should consider and record the extent and/or scope of their services and also any limitations thereto, in order to meet 1.2(c) and (d). This should be useful to the following:

- Clients wishing to check whether a practice can deal with their legal matter.
- Other external persons such as referrers of work.
- Personnel, in particular those in client-facing roles.

Since, in most cases, it will be clients and potential clients who will be most interested in this provision, the requirements may be met through practices producing lists and details of their services in brochures or on their websites. Examples of special features which will often be detailed include the languages in which advice can be given, the availability of home visits and wheelchair access to offices.

Practices providing publicly funded services should list the contract categories that are offered and any policy that they may have on the acceptance of instructions given and any limitations to matter starts.

1.2(e) does not require all practices to market themselves actively, but rather that they should consider whether marketing activity is appropriate for their practice. Practices that are content with their current supply of work, or consider that instructions may need to be turned away because of excess demand, would not be expected to involve themselves in promotional activities that are likely to further increase the number of potential instructions. If a decision is made not to engage in active marketing, it must be documented in order to meet this requirement. On the other hand, a practice that, as part of its strategy, sets out a desire to develop all or some of its practice areas, would need to show that it has considered the necessary marketing activity required in order to achieve this goal.

It is a requirement that practices can provide evidence that they have considered the financial implications of their marketing strategy. This may include the establishment of financial objectives within the plans. A finance plan is best seen as a management overview of the financial implications of the strategy in question. It is separate from, but perhaps ancillary to, more detailed budgets.

Irrespective of the manner in which marketing is dealt with, the documentation relating to it should cover:

- the areas of work that a practice wishes to develop, expand, reduce or cease to provide;
- the benefits that a practice hopes to achieve from its marketing or promotional activity;
- any promotional methods that will be employed and who will be responsible for them; and
- a budget for promotional activities.

When creating the marketing section of the plan, some of the issues that practices may want to consider are:

- type, length and style of desired documentation;
- possible use of external advice;
- personnel involvement and communication of the plan to members of personnel;
- feasible marketing activity and its budget; and
- the most effective format of review.

There are a range of tools that practices can use to help them evaluate risk, as required by 1.2(f). Undertaking a SWOT (Strengths, Weaknesses, Opportunities and Threats) analysis can assist practices in understanding their practice and the risks associated with either meeting or failing to meet their objectives.

There are other forms of analysis that practices can undertake such as PEST (Political, Environment, Social and Technological), which focus on micro-environmental factors. Ideally, practices should undertake both a SWOT and a PEST analysis to help them analyse the risks.

Practices are free to select the most appropriate form of reporting on performance. The most commonly used method of regular reporting on performance is the use of key performance indicators (KPIs). KPIs are typically monitored on a monthly or quarterly basis and provide a means of measuring progress towards the fulfilment of objectives. The KPIs used should link directly to the objectives, if they are to be of value. Regular monitoring of progress will enable practices to allocate resources to support them in meeting their set objectives. Alternatively, the strategic plan may be reviewed at management meetings and the minutes of the meeting can form the report on performance.

Sole practitioners: The strategic plan should include information that clarifies the key objectives of a practice over the next 12 months. Issues such as whether a practice intends to grow, in relation to personnel or income, should be addressed.

For sole practitioners who wish to continue their practice in its current state and have considered how realistic this is in relation to the external environment, it would be acceptable for the strategic plan to be very concise and state that the objective is to continue in its current state and that all necessary resources are in place. However, it is worth considering whether it is appropriate to improve a practice in some manner in order to remain competitive and to retain its market position.

As part of the risk evaluation sole practitioners should include the risk of them being incapacitated for a significant length of time or dying unexpectedly. This information may be presented as part of 1.2(f) or in the business continuity plan.

Sole practitioners will not be required to document the following:

- procedures for regular reporting; and
- who is responsible for the plan.

Large practices: As part of a practice's strategy and business planning, particularly in defining target groups and geographical locations it can outline plans to promote access to its services by diverse groups, taking account of language, cultural background, religion and disability.

If equality, diversity and inclusion initiatives are part of a practice's strategy to win new business or to develop its existing client base, the strategy and business plan should identify ways in which the practice can participate in such activities in the local and wider community. Ideally, a practice should indicate the steps that have been taken towards reaching this goal. This could also be included as part of a practice's corporate social responsibility (CSR) policy in 1.4.

Assessment note: The Standard does not require that personnel must be consulted on the strategic plan or any other documentation described in this section. It is, however, increasingly regarded as good business practice to involve personnel in the planning process.

All personnel should understand the broad strategy of their practice. Where appropriate they should be able to describe how they contribute to meeting the objectives set out in the strategic plan. During interviews, assessors will verify whether a practice's strategy is understood by its personnel.

The contents of the strategic plan and associated documentation may be kept confidential and therefore practices do not have to disclose it to their assessor. In such circumstances, assessors will need to seek evidence of the existence and understanding of such plans by conducting interviews. Interviews are likely to be at partner or senior manager level as these are the types of personnel most likely to be involved in business strategy.

1.3 Practices *must* have a business continuity *plan*, which *must* include:

(a) an *evaluation* of potential risks that could lead to business interruption
(b) ways to reduce, avoid and/or transfer the risks
(c) key people relevant to the implementation of the *plan*
(d) a *procedure* to test the plan annually, to verify that it would be effective in the event of a business interruption.

Having a business continuity plan (BCP) is a key risk management tool and business continuity risks are specifically mentioned in Chapter 7 of the SRA Code of Conduct 2011.

When drafting a BCP, it is worth considering the skills needed to implement the plan and which members of personnel possess these skills. It is also vital that there are clear communication channels, so that personnel and clients can be informed of any business interruptions. An important part of a practice's BCP is likely to be the back-up and retrieval arrangements.

In addition, practices should consider what risks could realistically impact on the continuity of their business in light of their location. Examples of procedures that practices should consider implementing in order to manage the risks are as follows:

- How they initially assess the disruptive situation.
- The preferred method of protecting personnel, clients, equipment, information and records.
- How to report emergencies.
- How to warn personnel.
- An evacuation plan.
- How to decide whether or not to shut down operations.
- How to shut down operations.
- How internal and external communications are to be handled.

The next step is to assess the likelihood of a risk occurring and its impact. Following this process should help practices to prioritise the risks and decide upon how to mitigate these risks. When addressing 1.3(b), practices may wish to tabulate the information.

Testing the BCP is one of the most valuable and challenging aspects thereof. The purpose of testing the BCP is to identify possible weaknesses and to rectify these before a real incident occurs. Practices must document both the BCP and how it is tested.

There are a range of methods that practices can use to test the BCP. One of the most frequently used methods is desktop testing. This involves creating a scenario and asking participants to discuss the steps to be taken in accordance with the BCP.

In addition to the scheduled testing of the BCP, practices may draw upon their experiences of actual interruptions to their business within the last 12 months, the lessons learned from such interruptions and whether any changes were made to the BCP as a result.

Best practice is to keep copies of the BCP away from the office, such as at the homes of members of personnel and to include key information to facilitate a practice getting back to business as usual as soon as possible, including, for example, building insurance contact details.

The Law Society produces a free practice note in relation to business continuity, which can be found at **www.lawsociety.org.uk/advice/practice-notes/business-continuity**.

Sole practitioners: Sole practitioners should consider leaving a letter or other instructions with a fellow practitioner, if there are reciprocal arrangements, or a friend or relative, to deal with their wishes for the practice in the case of death or incapacity. Further information can be obtained from the Sole Practitioners Group and the SRA.

Large practices: Practices which have more than one office may wish to have a plan for each office, as the risks are likely to vary, particularly in relation to the geographical location of their offices.

Because of the size and complexity of large practices, it may be worth considering outsourcing the testing of the BCP to a specialist organisation that will simulate interruptions to practices and thoroughly test each aspect of the BCP.

Practices may have a procedure which tests key elements of the BCP on a rolling basis. For example, practices could, every six months, test a particular aspect of the BCP, such as IT and check how personnel respond to the same.

Assessment note: Practices will be required to produce documentary evidence of their BCP and will be asked about the factors that were taken into consideration when it was produced. Assessors will review the extent and scope of the plan, as well as the methods through which practices communicate it to personnel or enforce any requirements contained within it. In addition, assessors may interview those personnel who are responsible for the implementation of any of the actions outlined in the plan, to ensure that their roles and responsibilities are understood. Assessors will also look for evidence that the plan has been reviewed at least annually. Testing of the plan must also be documented and such documentation must be available to assessors to review.

1.4 Practices *should* have a *policy* in relation to *corporate social responsibility*.

This requirement is optional for practices. However, if a practice tenders for work, it is likely that prospective clients will expect to see such a policy showing how the practice operates in a responsible manner. Some of the issues that a practice may want to incorporate into its policy include:

- facilities;
- recycling;
- resources;
- travel; and
- pro bono and charitable work.

It may be of benefit to practices to include details of the policy on their website in order to communicate aspects of their culture to clients and the wider community.

Sole practitioners: Many sole practitioners contribute significantly to the community and attempt to minimise their impact on the environment. However, it is uncommon for sole practitioners to have a documented CSR policy, unless they undertake niche work and/or it is a requirement of a client.

Large practices: Large practices often find it beneficial to have a documented CSR policy as it helps to consolidate a broad range of the activities that they undertake and contributes to setting the culture of their practice. In addition, many clients require practices to have a CSR policy because they want to ensure that they work with responsible practices. This is particularly relevant to practices that tender for work.

It is considered good practice to address the following issues in the CSR policy:

- The environment.
- The local community.
- Charities.

Communication of the policy is often the most challenging aspect of this requirement and practices may wish to have a communications plan which sets out activities to raise awareness of the policy.

In addition, if a key client requires a CSR policy, practices may wish to link it to their reporting on performance as required in 1.2(g) by way of a key performance indicator.

Assessment note: As this is an optional requirement, assessors should not raise non-compliances against this requirement.

2 FINANCIAL MANAGEMENT

The purpose of the financial management section is to provide a framework to help manage key financial matters.

2.1 Practices *must* document the person who has overall responsibility for financial management.

The compliance officer for financial administration (COFA), as the person who plays a significant role in the financial management of a practice, should ordinarily be named as the person with responsibility for the overall financial management of a practice.

Sole practitioners: Sole practitioners do not need to document that they are responsible for financial management. However, they must be able to discuss the financial management of their practice.

Small and medium practices: It is likely that the person who has overall responsibility for the financial management of a practice is the COFA and this person should be named in the relevant documentation. It is acceptable to name the role rather than the individual, i.e. to state that the COFA is responsible for overall financial management of a practice. Assessors will gather information to confirm that the person with overall financial responsibility of the practice has a clearly defined role and that other personnel understand when to contact the COFA. For example, if personnel are aware of a breach of a practice's financial policies or procedures.

Large practices: Practices may have a financial committee that is responsible for a range of financial management issues across their practice. As practices are required to identify a person, it is possible to name the COFA or person that chairs the committee. However, it is also acceptable to name the position, rather than the individual in the documentation.

Assessment note: Practices may reference the person with responsibility for overall financial management in an organisational chart or office manual. Alternatively, the information may be found on the intranet or within a job description. Assessors must accept the format chosen by practices to evidence this requirement.

2.2 Practices *must* be able to provide documentary evidence of their financial management *procedure*, including:

(a) annual budget including income and expenditure
(b) annual income and expenditure accounts
(c) annual balance sheet
(d) annual income and expenditure forecast to be reviewed quarterly
(e) variance analysis conducted at least quarterly of income and expenditure against budgets
(f) variance analysis conducted at least quarterly of cash flow and cash flow forecast.

Practices need to provide their assessor with documentary evidence to confirm that they produce the financial management information set out in the requirements of 2.2. There are essentially two methods of achieving this. Practices may provide their assessor with copies of their financial reports or alternatively, a letter from their accountant to confirm that they produce the necessary information.

Budgets are a means of communicating to managers the resources available to deliver their services. Budgets are most commonly expressed in financial terms. However, practices may wish to include non-financial terms, such as the number of clients they wish to deliver their services to. Budgets are also a crucial part of a practice's planning and control mechanism. Ideally, they should forecast not simply what is expected, but also what practices want to achieve.

2.2(a) does not prescribe how to budget, only that budgeting must be carried out. Therefore, practices should consider their circumstances and then decide which method is most suitable for them. Three main approaches can be taken to budgeting.

Firstly, incremental budgeting, which essentially takes the previous year's budget as the starting point. Adjustments are then made by adding or subtracting on an incremental basis. Although this is a simple method of producing a budget, it often neglects to take into consideration changes to a practice's objectives or strategy.

Secondly, zero-based budgeting (often referred to as priority-based budgeting) creates budgets by identifying targets and establishing the resources required to meet those targets. Typically, managers need to make a case for their expenditure. This method of creating budgets is unlikely to be necessary on an annual basis and is often undertaken every three to five years, with incremental budgeting in the intervening periods.

Thirdly, rolling budgets which are set at the beginning of a period and are regularly checked and amended to take into account emerging patterns that occur over the period. As each month passes a new budget month is added. Therefore, a 12-month budget is always in place. Although this method of budgeting is heavily reliant on IT, it provides ongoing flexibility for managers to direct resources from one part of a practice to another. This method of budgeting is often favoured during times of uncertainty.

The annual balance sheet is sometimes referred to as the statement of financial position and is a means by which an accountant represents where practices derive their funds from and where they use them.

The variance analysis that is referred to in 2.2(e) and (f) relates to the difference between the budgeted/forecast figures and the actual figures. Conducting the variance analysis will assist practices in understanding whether or not they are meeting their financial budgets and targets. Lexcel requires this to be done annually. However, there may be some practices where it would be more appropriate to conduct the variance analysis on a monthly basis.

> **Assessment note:** Assessors must receive documentation to satisfy the requirements in 2.2. As this data could be sensitive, it is acceptable for practices to provide a letter confirming that they produce the necessary financial information. Ideally the letter should be from a practice's accountant and specifically refer to the requirements in 2.2(a)–(f).

2.3 Practices *should* have a time recording *procedure*.

Time recording is an optional requirement and a non-compliance will not be raised if practices do not meet this requirement. However, if practices bill clients on a time basis it is crucial to accurately record time.

If practices do not bill clients on a time basis, they may wish to consider time recording, as it can provide useful management information in relation to productivity and profitability. If practices decide not to time record, it is prudent to conduct some form of analysis of departmental profitability, for example, by calculating the expenditure against the income of the department on a regular basis.

> **Assessment note:** This is an optional requirement and therefore assessors will not raise a non-compliance against 2.3. However, assessors may suggest that a practice implements time recording to assist with managing personnel.

2.4 Practices *must* have a *procedure* in relation to billing clients, which *must* include:

- **(a) the frequency and terms for billing clients**
- **(b) credit limits for new and existing clients**
- **(c) debt management.**

Practices may wish to set out their procedures by department or area of law in relation to 2.4(a) and (b). For example, the frequency and terms of billing clients in conveyancing matters may differ vastly from what is usual in litigation matters. This information must be conveyed to the client to ensure that expectations are managed from the outset of the matter.

Practices should consider occasions where fee earners may need to vary the procedures and set out from whom they must seek permission before acting.

Credit limits in 2.4(b) usually refer to the value of work that practices are willing to undertake before issuing their client with a bill. It is acceptable to set out a general procedure for all clients or matter types or decide this on a case-by-case basis.

2.4(c) requires practices to set out the steps to be taken in the event that a bill is not paid on time.

Communication between the accounts personnel and fee earners should be clear and effective to ensure that clients receive a consistent service, in the event that practices need to evoke their debt recovery procedure.

> **Assessment note:** Assessors will audit compliance with the requirement at 2.4 by reviewing the written procedure and interviewing personnel in order to ascertain if the procedure is understood and adhered to by personnel. In addition, assessors may also seek evidence on the matter files to understand whether the procedure works in practice.

2.5 Practices handling financial transactions *must* have a *procedure* which *must* include:

(a) the transfer of funds
(b) the management of funds received by the practice
(c) *authorisations*.

Practices must ensure that their procedures take into consideration the SRA Accounts Rules, particularly in relation to office and client funds as well as mixed money.

Details of how financial transactions are authorised must be encompassed within the procedure. It will be for practices to decide how best to present and communicate to personnel the procedure required at 2.5.

> **Assessment note:** Assessors will audit compliance against 2.5 by reviewing the written procedure and interviewing personnel in order to ascertain if the procedure is understood and adhered to by personnel. In addition, assessors may also seek evidence on the matter files to assess whether the procedure works in practice.

3 INFORMATION MANAGEMENT

3.1 Practices *must* have an information management and security *policy*, which *must* include:

(a) a *register* of relevant information assets of both the practice and clients
(b) *procedures* for the protection and security of the information assets
(c) *procedures* for the retention and disposal of information
(d) the use of firewalls
(e) *procedures* for the secure configuration of network devices
(f) *procedures* to manage user accounts
(g) *procedures* to detect and remove *malicious software*
(h) a *register* of all software used by the practice
(i) training for *personnel* on information security
(j) a *plan* for the updating and monitoring of software.

When drafting the policy, practices will need to decide the scope of the policy and be clear about what they want the policy to achieve. Practices may wish to use the opportunity to reflect on the effectiveness of their current approach and develop a policy that will support their strategic direction. Alternatively practices may consider their approach to be robust and simply want to reflect it in the policy. It is important to also consider the influence of the policy on other aspects of their practice. For example, how does IT support the information systems that are in place? The policy must also set clear boundaries for personnel to operate within and explain the potential consequences if the policy is not adhered to.

Some of the key issues that the information management and security policy needs to address are how practices ensure that information is kept confidential, its integrity is maintained and that it is accessible. This is critical to practices on a day-to-day basis and also needs to be considered in the context of the business continuity requirements that are set out in 1.3. The policy must encompass information that is held electronically and physically.

Often the register will include the following main headings:

- The title.
- An identifier or unique reference number.
- A description.
- The date created.
- The frequency it is to be updated (e.g. monthly, annually).
- The date it was last modified.
- The format (e.g. word document, book).
- The author.
- The users' rights (e.g. rights to view, copy, redistribute or republish).
- The category (e.g. confidential, personal data).
- Retention period.
- Destruction date.

Lexcel does not, however, prescribe the format of the register and practices have the freedom to decide how best to capture the information.

Large practices managing a significant number of information assets may have a dedicated database which serves as the register.

Smaller practices may create the register using an Excel spreadsheet, if there is a smaller volume of information to manage.

To create the information asset register as required by 3.1(a), practices need to define what an information asset is. One method practices may wish to consider adopting is to analyse the value of the information by assessing the impact its loss would have. This should help practices decide whether the information is an asset and needs to be included in the register. Practices need to ensure that both their assets and those of their clients are included in the register. Keeping a register will also help to achieve requirements set out in 3.1(b). Once practices understand the likelihood and impact of risks to their information assets, they can then take steps to mitigate those risks.

There are some risks that change very quickly, particularly in relation to information that is held electronically. Therefore, practices are encouraged to regularly review the procedures adopted to meet 3.1(b) as threats change. The government has introduced the Cyber Essentials Scheme to help businesses deal with cyber security issues. To find out more information about the scheme, go to **www.gov.uk/government/publications/cyber-essentials-scheme-overview**.

The Law Society also provides an online training course, which deals with cyber security issues. This free online training can be accessed at **http://cpdcentre.lawsociety.org.uk/course/6707/cyber-security-for-legal-and-accountancy-professionals**.

In addition, there is an international standard for information security, ISO 27001, to which practices may wish to consider aligning or gaining accreditation. More information is available at **www.iso.org/iso/home/standards/management-standards/iso27001.htm**.

When practices are formulating their policy in relation to 3.1(c), they should ensure that it is consistent with the file retention periods required by 4.5(e) and 7.6(f). Practices may wish to include the retention and destruction dates as part of the information asset register. Care should be taken to ensure that the policy is consistent with current data protection legislation. Practices may wish to access the Law Society's practice note on data protection, available at **www.lawsociety.org.uk/advice/practice-notes/data-protection**.

The policy must also address the issue of firewalls, as set out in 3.1(d), as this plays a key role in the ability of practices to safeguard information assets. A firewall is a barrier which protects the network or computer from unauthorised access and can filter incoming and outgoing information which may be harmful. Practices need to ensure that the firewalls in use are appropriate and regularly updated.

Technology plays a key role in helping to secure a practice's network. 3.1(e) should set the parameters for personnel within the practice to work within and ideally they should include procedures that deal with the following:

- Use of strong passwords.
- Hiding any network ID.
- Use of encryption.

The procedures required for 3.1(f), to manage user accounts should specify a practice's approach to the following issues:

- Application settings.
- User data folder.
- Security privileges and policy settings.
- File system permissions.

Having procedures to detect and remove malicious software, to meet 3.1(g), is crucial to having a robust approach to information security. Clearly IT software plays a role in protecting practices but practices require procedures to deal with malicious software, for example identifying the anti-malware that is going to be most suitable for a practice. Typically the practice should set out the frequency that the network is checked for malware. As cyber criminals are constantly developing new malware it is necessary to have procedures in place to minimise the risk of falling prey to cyber attacks. In the event that the practice outsources the management of its IT, it must ensure that it sets out the procedures for the supplier to operate within.

All software used by practices needs to be included in a register, in order to comply with 3.1(h). This will assist practices with managing software programs and ensuring that only approved software is in use.

One of the key weaknesses in any organisation's armour in respect of threats is personnel not understanding the policy and allowing threats to bypass the safeguards that have been put in place. Training personnel to a high standard should ensure that they understand the policy and provide a robust defence to potential threats. For example practices may have very effective firewalls, but, if social engineering techniques enable a criminal to persuade a member of personnel to insert a memory stick into their computer and unwittingly introduce malware, the investment in technology would have been somewhat wasted.

Software often changes at a rapid rate, which enables new methods of working. 3.1(j) requires that a plan is in place to ensure that future software needs are understood and that appropriate budgets are set aside to fulfil such plan.

There are also Law Society practice notes on information security and cloud computing that practices may wish to consider.

They can be accessed at the following:

- **www.lawsociety.org.uk/advice/practice-notes/information-security.**
- **www.lawsociety.org.uk/advice/practice-notes/cloud-computing.**

Assessment note: The assessor will review the documented policy and gather interview evidence to confirm that it is understood and in effective operation.

3.2 Practices *must* have an e-mail *policy*, which *must* include:

(a) the scope of permitted and prohibited use
(b) *procedures* for monitoring *personnel* using e-mail
(c) *procedures* for the storage and destruction of e-mails.

The e-mail policy may be part of a general communication policy or be part of the information management and security policy. The e-mail policy will be Lexcel compliant, provided that the issues in 3.2(a), (b) and (c) are addressed. The scope of the policy should address e-mails at a systems and individual level. The systems level should address issues such as the supplier and mailbox limits and the provision for encryption. For example, is the e-mail system a commercial off the shelf software or open source software? The individual level should set out the behaviours that a practice requires of personnel, such as using e-mail for business purposes only. Practices must take steps to ensure that personnel are trained to understand the policy and understand the consequences of failing to adhere to the policy. It is considered prudent for practices to ensure that personnel understand the policy and will abide by it. This may form part of a contract of employment or the induction.

One of the most challenging aspects of the e-mail policy is the monitoring of personnel. 3.2(b) does not require a practice to monitor e-mails, only that it sets out what its policy is in relation to monitoring. Therefore, practices may or may not choose to monitor e-mails. This information should be communicated to personnel via the policy.

In the event that a practice does monitor personnel e-mails, it should be mindful of privacy issues and ensure that it takes a proportionate approach and takes steps to ensure that personnel are aware that it monitors e-mails. Care must be taken to comply with current regulations. Practices may wish to consult the Information Commissioner's guidance on monitoring employee e-mails to ensure that their policy is in compliance with relevant legislation.

When a practice defines its policy in relation to 3.2(c), it should consider whether it is consistent with 3.1(c), 4.5(e) and 7.6(f) that deal with the archiving and destruction of files.

Sole practitioners: For a sole practitioner with no staff, and no support staff, it is not necessary to document 3.2(a) and (b). However, sole practitioners will need to ensure there is a documented procedure for the storage and destruction of e-mails. In the event of a sole practitioner being unexpectedly absent, this information would be of benefit to those taking over the management of his or her practice.

Small and medium practices: Practices should ensure that their policy clearly sets out the boundaries that personnel are expected to work within. Ideally 3.2(a) should address the following:

- Whether or not e-mail may be used to send personal e-mails.
- The type of information that may and may not be sent by e-mail.
- The use of attachments (e.g. should letters containing advice be sent as an attachment or is it acceptable to send advice to clients in the body of e-mails).
- What to do in the event that a practice receives a suspicious e-mail or attachment.

There are a range of methods practices could adopt to monitor e-mails. One arrangement may be that supervisors have access to the e-mail accounts of those that they supervise. Alternatively there is software available to assist with monitoring e-mails, which may be of benefit, if practices consider the volume of e-mails to be high and challenging to monitor in any other way.

Large practices: The high volume of e-mail traffic may necessitate the use of software to assist in monitoring e-mails, should a practice decide to do so. It is likely that practices will have a dedicated person or team that will develop and support the policy. If the IT staff have concerns that the e-mail policy isn't being adhered to, the policy should set out how they raise their concerns with the partners/directors/management team.

Assessment note: Assessors will review the documented policy and gather interview evidence to confirm that the policy is understood and adhered to.

3.3 If the practice has a website, the practice *must* have a website management *policy*, which *must* include:

(a) a *procedure* for content approval, publishing and removal
(b) the scope of permitted and prohibited content
(c) *procedures* for the management of its security
(d) consideration of accessibility requirements for disabled clients.

Before drafting its website policy a practice should consider what the purpose of the website is, for example, does it want its website to simply promote its practice or be an interactive site and a means of delivering legal services? Practices should also ensure that the policy addresses website issues at a system and individual level.

3.3(a) is primarily focused on the systems level and requires a practice to consider issues concerning how content for the website will be approved, published and removed. Roles and responsibilities as well as the budget should be considered at this stage. The procedures should include a check to ensure that the website is fulfilling the needs of the end user, for example, has the website's usability been tested? It is also critical to ensure that a practice's website is compliant from a legal and regulatory perspective. Therefore, the policy should include the following issues:

- Copyright.
- Data protection.
- Defamation.
- SRA Code of Conduct, Chapter 8, Publicity.
- Electronic commerce.
- Distance selling.
- Equality and diversity.

Practices will need to provide guidance to personnel that are involved in the creation and updating of the website. 3.3(b) requires practices to provide guidance to personnel that are involved in the creation and updating of the website.

The requirement at 3.3(c) must be consistent with the information management and security policy. This may form part of such policy or be part of a general communications policy. Lexcel does not set out a particular format that should be used, only that the requirement must be complied with. A practice will need to set out the steps it has in place to safeguard the confidentiality of the website data, for example, whether contractors are able to access confidential data stored by the website.

The integrity of a practice's website is another strand to the security of its website that needs to be incorporated into the policy. Technical safeguards need to be in place to prevent attackers being able to make changes to the website, as well as effectively managing issues such as disabling former employees' access, so that they can no longer make changes to the website. Increasingly, practices need to be vigilant and check their online presence, as some practices have had their website cloned or have had members of personnel appear on bogus firms' websites. Regularly checking the internet will help alert a practice to the misuse of its website, should it occur.

One of the most frequent types of attack on websites revolves around them being taken offline. Practices may wish to access the Department for Business, Innovation and Skills' *10 Steps to Cyber Security* for additional guidance on information security and websites.

Practices must consider the needs of disabled clients and potential clients and take all reasonable steps to ensure that the website is accessible to them. The requirement at 3.3(d) may be addressed as part of a practice's equality and diversity policy or as part of the website management policy. Again, Lexcel provides flexibility in how a practice meets the requirements.

Assessment note: 3.3 does not make it mandatory for practices to have a website, but if they do, it is necessary to establish a policy that meets all of the requirements in 3.3(a)–(d).

Assessors will review the documented policy, view the website and gather interview evidence to verify whether the policy is in effective operation.

3.4 Practices *must* have an internet access *policy*, which *must* include:

(a) the scope of permitted and prohibited use
(b) *procedures* for monitoring *personnel* accessing the internet.

The internet is a powerful business tool for research in areas of interest to personnel. The policy should assist personnel in understanding what is deemed appropriate use. 3.4(a) requires boundaries of use to be set for personnel. Practices will want staff to use the internet in a proper and appropriate manner, including compliance with core policies on areas such as discrimination and the downloading of offensive material. The policy will need to reflect the culture of a practice, for example, setting out whether personnel are permitted to access the internet for personal use during lunch breaks or whether the internet may only be used for business purposes.

As with the e-mail policy, it is considered good practice to incorporate the internet use policy into conditions of employment and include it as part of the induction. This helps to ensure that all personnel are aware of and understand the policy. In addition, practices may want to set out the potential penalties for misuse.

3.4(b) does not require practices to monitor personnel accessing the internet. However, the policy must state whether or not the practice monitors internet use. If a practice chooses to monitor internet use, then it must ensure that it considers an individual's right to privacy and it must take a proportional approach. There is the possibility of using software to assist with monitoring. Practices may wish to access further guidance in relation to monitoring personnel by visiting the Information Commissioner's Office website, to help ensure that the policy complies with current legislation and good practice (**http://ico.org.uk**).

This policy may form part of the information security and information management policy or be a standalone policy. Issues such as downloading information and programs should be addressed in the policy.

Sole practitioners: It is not necessary to document the internet access policy for sole practitioners with no fee earning or support personnel. However, if a practice does have personnel, it must have a written policy which sets out the scope of permitted and prohibited use. This usually includes whether personnel may access the internet for personal use or may only use it for work-related activities. In addition, the policy should include specific examples of what would constitute a breach of the policy, for example, accessing pornography.

Small and medium practices: The purpose of the policy is to set boundaries for personnel. The policy must include a named person or role that is responsible for the policy and the review of the policy. The policy must be reviewed at least annually; however the practice may wish to review it more frequently.

Large practices: Large practices may have a specialist person or team that deals with the IT aspects of the internet access policy and other electronic communication and information policies. However, in order for the policies to be fully effective, a senior member of management needs to be available to deal with managerial aspects of the policy and ensure that the IT aspects align with the practice's strategy.

Assessment note: Assessors will review the documented policy and gather interview evidence to confirm that it is understood and in effective operation.

3.5 Practices *must* have a social media *policy*, which *must* include:

(a) a *procedure* for participating in social media on behalf of the practice
(b) the scope of permitted and prohibited content.

As with all policies, a good starting point is to consider what a practice wants the policy to achieve. The social media policy should also be consistent with the policy at 3.1. Social media is a dynamic form of communication and the policy will need to reflect the level of access to members of personnel. For example, whether a practice encourages all personnel to participate in social media to raise its profile or if there are designated personnel that are permitted to participate on its behalf. Clear guidelines need to be set out and understood by all staff members. It is likely that a practice would want social media to enhance its reputation and avoid potential damage to the same. Therefore the policy should address key issues, such as:

- the scope of the policy;
- roles and responsibilities;
- forms of social media;
- how the policy applies to business and personal use;
- consequences of breaching the policy; and
- how to give feedback on the policy.

As with other policies, it is considered good practice to incorporate the social media policy into conditions of employment and include it as part of the induction. This helps to ensure that all personnel are aware of and understand the policy. In addition, practices may want to set out the potential penalties for misuse.

Sole practitioners: Sole practitioners with no members of personnel do not need to document the requirements of 3.5. However, sole practitioners may wish to link their social media policy with their strategic plan, which is required in 1.2.

Small and medium practices: It is necessary to name the person or role that is responsible for the social media policy and ensure that the policy is reviewed at least annually.

Practices may wish to consider how their social media policy aligns with their strategic plan in 1.2 and ensure there are no conflicts between them.

The policy should set out who is able to participate in social media on behalf of a practice and the scope of permitted and prohibited content. For example, the information should be accurate and not damage the practice's reputation.

Large practices: Large practices may wish to host workshops with a cross-section of personnel to discuss social media issues. It is likely that these practices will have dedicated personnel to participate in social media on their behalf and they will need guidance to help them fulfil their role.

3.6 Practices *must* have:

(a) a *register* of each *plan, policy* and *procedure* that is contained in the Lexcel Standard
(b) a named person responsible for each *policy, plan* and *procedure* that is contained in the Lexcel Standard
(c) a *procedure* for the review of each *policy, plan* and *procedure* that is contained in the Lexcel Standard.

The requirements of 3.6 apply to all plans, policies and procedures in sections 1 to 7 of the Standard. Generally, the register will include the following information:

- The name of the person responsible.
- The name of the document.
- The date that the document was created.
- The date that the document was last updated.
- The frequency of review.

Issues that practices may wish to include in the review procedure are as follows:

- Whether there have been any breaches.
- Whether there have been any near breaches.
- Whether the law or regulations have changed in this area.
- Whether lines of accountability or reporting have changed.
- Whether a practice is satisfied that the plan, policy or procedure is fit for purpose.

Sole practitioners: It is not necessary for sole practitioners to document 3.6(a) or (b). However, 3.6(c) is concerned with continuous improvement and the procedure for review should be documented.

Large practices: There may be a committee that takes responsibility for particular plans, policies or procedures. It is acceptable for practices to name the committee, rather than an individual if the responsibility is dealt with in this manner. It is also possible to name a role rather than a person in order to comply with 3.6(b).

Assessment note: Assessors will check that the register includes all policies, plans and procedures across the Standard. There may be instances where one of a practice's policies deals with several Lexcel policies. For example, the information management and security policy may encompass the e-mail, internet use and social media policy. Practices will be required to ensure that the information in the register is sufficiently detailed to communicate the roles and reviews associated with each policy.

4 PEOPLE MANAGEMENT

4.1 Practices *must* have a *policy* in relation to the health and safety of all *personnel* and visitors to the practice.

There are legal duties on employers and organisations to ensure a safe working environment. In accordance with the applicable legislation, practices should adopt a policy to ensure that they are taking adequate steps to meet their obligations. A good source of information is the Health and Safety Executive's website (**www.hse.gov.uk**).

Practices should take steps to ensure that their policy sets out their commitment to managing health and safety effectively and what they intend to achieve. It should be apparent from the policy who is responsible for the policy and the specific actions required to meet the practice's obligations.

In addition, practices should provide details of the steps that they propose to take to achieve the aims set out in their health and safety policy.

When drafting a health and safety policy, practices may wish to consider the following issues:

- Equipment.
- The handling and use of substances by personnel.
- Accidents, first aid and work-related ill health.
- Monitoring of conditions and systems of work.
- Emergency procedures, fire and evacuation of premises.
- Home working.
- Lone working.
- Meeting clients away from the office.
- Stress management.
- Visitors to their premises, including clients and third parties.

Sole practitioners: Sole practitioners that have fewer than five employees are not obliged to document their health and safety policy under legislation. However, for Lexcel purposes such practices must document their health and safety policy unless they have no personnel.

Small and medium practices: Practices with fewer than five employees are not obliged to document their health and safety policy under legislation. However, for Lexcel purposes such practices must document their health and safety policy.

> **Assessment note:** Assessors must verify that the documented policy is congruent with interview evidence from personnel.
>
> For sole practitioners without any personnel, assessors will only seek interview evidence to confirm compliance with the health and safety policy.

4.2 Practices *must* have an equality and diversity *policy*, which *must* include:

(a) recruitment, selection and progression
(b) a *procedure* to deal with complaints and disciplinary issues in breach of the *policy*
(c) a *procedure* to monitor diversity and collate equality data
(d) training of all *personnel* on compliance with equality and diversity requirements
(e) *procedures* for *reasonable adjustments* for *personnel*.

Equal opportunities and anti-discrimination are concepts concerned with providing opportunities and removing barriers that affect particular groups. Legislation is increasingly protecting the rights of people in various groups in society and prohibits discrimination on the grounds of racial or ethnic origin, disability, age, gender, sexual orientation and religion or belief. Anti-discrimination legislation is designed to promote equality and fairness in relation to employment and the provision of services.

Diversity is a broader concept that builds upon the progress made through equal opportunities. Policies must encourage the development of individuals regardless of their background and irrespective of social class and education. Diversity promotes the recognition of the value that each person can bring to the workplace.

A practice's equality and diversity policy must cover recruitment, selection, progression, retention and pay. Practices should have regard to outcome 2.4 of the SRA Code of Conduct, principle 9 of the SRA Principles and equality legislation to ensure that their policy is effective.

The policy should cover both existing and new personnel and should be made available to all personnel in a practice. This can be achieved by publishing it on the practice's website or by making it a part of the practice's manual or an induction/ introductory pack provided to all personnel.

Practices should monitor their equality and diversity policy on a regular basis to ensure it is being complied with. This review must take place at least annually.

An annual survey, whether online or manual, can help practices to collect diversity data. The SRA has issued a model questionnaire to be used for the collection of diversity data, which can be found on the SRA's website.

It is mandatory for practices to survey their personnel. However, individual members of personnel are under no obligation to disclose their data. They can state that they would prefer not to say and should not be forced or pressurised to provide data. However it is considered to be good practice to encourage personnel to complete the survey.

Practices must also publish the diversity data that they have collected but only where doing so does not breach confidentiality. This means that where there is a small group of personnel (e.g. fewer than 10) in any given diversity category, a practice should only publish if it has the explicit consent of everyone who has provided the data. Practices may choose the form in which they publish the data, for example, on their website, as a printed handout or on a notice in the reception area. The key issue is ensuring that it is readily available.

The collected diversity data should be used by practices to analyse the composition of their workforce, by diversity, in comparison to relevant baseline data (for example data from the Law Society on the diversity profile of the profession and official diversity statistics on the working age profile in the practice area/region in which they are based) and to identify any under-representation. Practices should also use the data to review their recruitment, selection and promotion procedures to ensure that these are fair and that under-represented groups are encouraged to apply.

Diversity training must be provided to all personnel. Such training must set out the equality and diversity requirements and inform personnel about their individual and collective duties.

Practices must be aware of their obligations to ensure reasonable adjustments are made for disabled employees in accordance with outcome 2.3 of the SRA Code of Conduct 2011 and principle 9 of the SRA Principles. The equality and diversity policy should set out what steps the practice intends to take to identify and manage reasonable adjustment requests from personnel who have a disability. A list of the types of adjustment the practice can offer may be included in the policy.

Practices should ensure that the policy includes a consideration of the following issues:

- Discrimination in employment.

  Equal opportunities, anti-discrimination and diversity work together by addressing the inequalities and barriers faced by people, as well as by valuing, learning from and benefiting from the diverse cultures in society. Employees have a right to expect fair and equal treatment. This expectation is supported by the law. Discrimination can deny practices access to the widest range of talent. In addition, fair treatment makes good business sense, as employers who treat employees fairly and flexibly will be best placed to recruit and retain staff in an increasingly diverse and competitive labour market.

Unlawful discrimination can be costly to a practice, as there is no limit to the damages that an employment tribunal can require a practice to pay to a claimant, if the practice is found to have discriminated against an employee. Employers are also vicariously responsible for the actions of their employees and so it is important, therefore, that employees know what is expected of them.

- Discrimination in the provision of services.

  Practices are generally free to decide whether to accept instructions from a particular client. However, any refusal to act must not be based upon discriminatory grounds.

  Practices should maintain lists of experts and third parties who are regarded as suitable for instruction. A practice should ensure that the lists are compiled on the basis of the ability of those listed to undertake work of a particular type. The list should not exclude, restrict or make any preference on discriminatory grounds as set out in the Standard and legislation.

  Practices may develop different policies to address anti-discrimination, equality and diversity or have one main policy. For the anti-discrimination and equal opportunities policy to be effective, it must have the support of everyone in the practice and be an integral part of the business strategy. The involvement of senior managers is vital in order to show commitment to the policy.

Sole practitioners: The collection and reporting of diversity data from practices is a mandatory requirement imposed by the SRA. This is the case even if a sole practitioner is the only person that is working within the practice and there are no personnel.

Small and medium practices: Small to medium sized practices must publish the diversity data that they have collected but only where in doing so they do not breach confidentiality. This means that where there is a small group of personnel (e.g. fewer than 10) in any given diversity category, practices should only publish if they have the explicit consent of everyone who has provided the data. Practices may choose the form in which they publish the data, for example on their website, as a printed handout or a notice in the reception area. The key issue is ensuring that it is readily available.

Large practices: Large practices may have an equality and diversity committee/working group to help them implement their policy and communicate their commitment to equality and diversity.

Practices should deliver a range of equality and diversity training and information which is suitable for the variety of personnel within the practice.

Practices should use trained staff to review the effect of their policies and ensure that such reviews are documented. Where relevant, practices may undertake an equality impact assessment (EIA) on key policies.

Practices should use the collected workforce diversity data to monitor key functions such as recruitment, selection, promotion, grievances and training. Where a practice has identified under-representation on diversity grounds in its recruitment or promotion data, it can put a positive action programme in place to help to improve diversity in its workforce including at senior level.

Practices may wish to undertake a full disability access audit and have an access action plan in place.

Assessment note: Assessors will review the documented policy and gather interview evidence to verify that the policy is understood by personnel. In addition, audit trails may be followed to gather evidence that the policy is in operation. For example, assessors may request sight of records pertaining to recruitment, selection and progression within practices. Assessors may also request sight of records that demonstrate that the procedures to deal with complaints and disciplinary issues are being adhered to. Assessors may also wish to review the equality and diversity monitoring data to assess how the procedures in 4.2(c) are working. Assessors must ensure that they have permission from personnel to have sight of their records.

4.3 Practices *must* have a learning and development *policy*, which *must* include:

(a) ensuring that appropriate training is provided to *personnel* within the practice
(b) ensuring that all *supervisors* and managers receive appropriate training
(c) a *procedure* to evaluate training
(d) a learning and development *plan* for all *personnel*.

Ensuring that a practice's personnel are appropriately trained will assist it to thrive. The policy should encompass the key areas that the practice considers vital to its success, for example client care. The learning and development policy should provide all staff with an outline of the extent of the policy and the options available to them, including any restrictions identified by the practice. Practices should consider detailing any financial or resource limitations to any training.

Effective learning and development policies can prove invaluable to practices by promoting the development of members of personnel. This can support personnel retention activities as well as being a means to ensure that clients are aware of the practice's commitment to improve the quality of its services/products.

Supervisors and managers will be required to undertake some form of supervision/management training. The type and frequency of the training will be determined by the needs of a practice and should align with its business strategy.

Each person within a practice has a set of skills and by understanding the current level of skills and knowledge of personnel, practices can address any gaps and incorporate them into a learning and development plan, as required by 4.3(d).

4.4 Practices *must* list the tasks to be undertaken by all *personnel* within the practice usually in the form of a *role profile*.

A role profile details the essential and required/desired skills, knowledge, and experience necessary for a particular role or post. A job description details the tasks and responsibilities of a position. It is commonplace for the role profile and job description to be contained within the same document.

All personnel within the practice, regardless of status, must have a role profile or similar documentation in place. The precise format of the job documentation will be at the discretion of a practice, but typically it should include the job title and then cover the jobholder's place within the practice, reporting lines, the main purpose(s) of the role and a list of specific responsibilities.

It is good practice to review the job skills, knowledge, experience and the description regularly. Many practices do so at the appraisal meeting of each individual member of personnel, especially as it enables a review of the role over a suitably long timescale.

Sole practitioners: It is not necessary for sole practitioners to have a documented role profile. However, if there are any personnel, sole practitioners must ensure that such personnel have a role profile or similar document that sets out the tasks to be undertaken.

Assessment note: Assessors may request to see the documentation associated with any job within the practice. Where this includes documents relating to an individual's appraisal, consent from the individual must be sought first.

4.5 Practices *must* have *procedures* to deal effectively with recruitment selection and progression, which *must* include:

(a) the identification of vacancies
(b) the drafting of the job documentation
(c) methods of attracting candidates
(d) clear and transparent selection
(e) storage, retention and destruction of records
(f) references and ID checking
(g) where appropriate, the checking of disciplinary records.

Effective recruitment into a practice should significantly improve the quality of the service that it provides and reduce the risks associated with recruiting. Recruitment and selection must be a transparent process which is seen to be as objective and non-discriminatory as possible. In many practices there will be different arrangements for the recruitment and selection of different types of personnel, such as fee earners, trainees and secretaries. Ensuring that practices have effective recruitment procedures in place should assist them in recruiting the most suitable person for a vacancy. The procedures must include both those used internally by practices and those that are outsourced to recruitment agencies. Inclusive language must be used. The processes should be supported by having a formal and transparent process in relation to promotion and progression within a practice. This may include clear role specifications for all role types and scoring candidates on essential and desirable criteria based on experience and which can be demonstrated in the application and interview process.

It is considered good practice to consider interview questions in advance of the interview and to document them. This can help to ensure that practices gather as much information as possible during the interview and reduces the likelihood of forgetting to ask relevant questions or asking inappropriate ones. Part of the interview process may include candidates being assessed in some way. The assessment could be designed to test their technical ability or personality profile.

Practices should maintain records of interview notes, at the very least to assist them in defending any potential claim of unfairness in the process. Practices should note that merely having notes of the interview will not in itself defend against a claim of unfair treatment or discrimination. To ensure equality in the recruitment process, practices should consider including criteria at relevant stages of the process, for example, interview criteria and interview assessment or score sheets.

The Employment Practices Data Protection Code (Part 1) provides that interview notes should not be kept for longer than one year.

Once a practice has selected the candidate that it would like to appoint, it must ensure that it vets the person by obtaining references, confirming his or her eligibility to work in the European Union and verifying his or her identity. In addition, it is worth considering obtaining proof of qualifications and a P45.

4.5(g) requires a practice to satisfy itself that the disciplinary records of a candidate or member of personnel are acceptable to it. It is for a practice to decide the means of conducting these checks. It may decide to contact the professional body for the candidate or member of personnel or obtain a signed declaration from the candidate or member of personnel confirming the status of his or her disciplinary record.

Sole practitioners: Sole practitioners that do not have any intentions to recruit and are the only person within the practice do not need to have documented procedures to address 4.5. However, if their intentions change, then they must set out their procedures in respect of 4.5, in advance of recruiting.

Assessment note: Practices must ensure that the requirements are documented. Assessors may look for evidence of such documentation and any other recruitment policies within a practice. Assessors may interview those within a practice who have been involved in the recruitment process, from both employer and employee perspectives. In addition, assessors may ask to see records of any recruitment campaigns carried out, subject to confidentiality.

4.6 Practices *must* conduct an appropriate induction for all *personnel*, including those transferring roles within the practice and *must* cover:

(a) the management structure and the individual's responsibilities
(b) terms and conditions of employment
(c) immediate training requirements
(d) key *policies*.

It is recognised that the full induction process may be staggered over a period of time and may consist of the provision of reading materials, face-to-face meetings or the use of interactive materials on a practice's intranet. The induction process may be varied, depending on the position of the recruit and whether they are temporary, permanent or transferring from within the practice.

The induction process is a good opportunity to ensure that the person is aware of the practice's culture and the standards expected of them. Furthermore it is necessary to explain the support structures available to personnel. This information may be presented in a variety of forms, such as an organisational chart.

The key policies that are typically communicated during induction include the following:

- Information security.
- E-mail and internet access.
- Social media.
- Health and safety.
- Equality and diversity.

- Risk management policy.
- Anti-money laundering policy (if applicable).
- Avoidance of mortgage fraud (if applicable).
- Anti-bribery.
- Client care.

Sole practitioners: Sole practitioners who decide to recruit anyone must ensure that they are appropriately inducted. 4.6 includes inducting temporary personnel, such as locums who may provide holiday cover.

Assessment note: There is no need to document how induction training is provided, but assessors will need to see sufficient evidence that the induction process is effective. Assessors may ask to see any records concerning induction and/or interview members of personnel who have had an induction recently, in order to ascertain compliance.

4.7 Practices *must* have a *procedure* which details the steps to be followed when a member of *personnel* ceases to be an employee, which *must* include:

(a) the handover of work
(b) exit interviews
(c) the return of property belonging to the practice.

The procedure referred to at 4.7(a) should include whether the person leaving needs to prepare notes for the person taking over their work. In addition, the procedure should state whether there is to be a handover period during which the member of personnel who is exiting and the person taking on the role work together.

The purpose of the exit interview is to find out what practices are doing well and what they could improve upon in the opinion of their employees. Below are some examples of questions practices may wish to include during exit interviews:

- What prompted you to seek a new job?
- Why are you leaving?
- Did you share your concerns with anyone prior to deciding to leave?
- What have you enjoyed about working here?
- What have you disliked about working here?
- How would you describe the supervision you received?
- Did you have adequate resources to fulfil your role?
- Do you have any suggestions as to how we could be a better employer?

It is acknowledged that it is not always possible or appropriate to conduct exit interviews, for example, where a member of personnel declines to attend an exit interview or is in the process of being made redundant or being dismissed.

In addition to ensuring that a practice's property is returned in accordance with 4.7(c), a practice should consider any steps that it should take to ensure that the information management and security policy set out in 3.1 is adhered to, for example, disabling access to the practice's network and disabling e-mail accounts. Property that often needs to be returned includes:

- laptops;
- mobile devices;
- fob keys to access the network remotely;
- keys; and
- cars.

Practices may find it beneficial to have a set of documents that includes checklists and interview questions to assist with staff leaving procedures.

Sole practitioners: Sole practitioners who do not have any personnel do not need to document the procedures as set out in 4.7.

Assessment note: Assessors will request exit interview records to confirm that such procedures are working effectively. Practices may not have the permission of former members of personnel to share exit interview information, particularly if it contains personal information. Therefore, practices should, as a matter of course, seek permission of members of personnel to share the exit interview documentation with an assessor as part of the procedures.

4.8 Practices *must* have a performance management *policy*, which *must* include:

(a) the practice's approach to performance management
(b) performance review periods and timescales.

The performance management policy should include the following information:

- How performance is reviewed.
- Further development of personnel.
- Set objectives that should align with the practice's strategic plan (see 1.2).
- Available support and resources.
- Training needs.

Where personnel are involved in activities that support a practice's equality and diversity policy, these activities should be reflected appropriately in individual performance management reviews.

The requirement in this section for written records and documented procedures is to ensure that any relevant issues are addressed. Written records of the discussions and agreements emerging from the process are vital to its effectiveness.

Reviews can take a variety of forms, for example mentoring, appraisals or score card systems. An effective review scheme is essential to the performance management programme of most practices. This does not necessarily mean, however, that the same documentation should be in use for all personnel or that the process should be unduly bureaucratic. Partners and directors, in particular, may be subject to quite different arrangements from other personnel within a practice.

In most practices the setting of objectives will coincide with the annual review, but this does not necessarily have to be the case. It is commonplace for financial objectives emerging from the budget, for example, to be settled before the start of the financial year and then reviewed in appraisal meetings, or ongoing departmental or office meetings. It is good practice to consider individual objectives in relation to the overall business objectives for the forthcoming year.

It is common practice to review training needs for jobholders within review meetings, possibly in conjunction with other training reviews throughout the year. This information should, therefore, assist with generating a training plan.

Performance review records are sensitive and will need to be subject to controls under data protection compliance considerations. Practices should make clear who has access to records and for how long they are to be retained.

Sole practitioners: Sole practitioners that do not have any personnel do not need to have a documented performance management policy. However, such practices may wish to align their performance objectives with their strategic plan and measure their performance based on achieving the strategic objectives as required in 1.2. Alternatively, sole practitioners may wish to seek external support by way of a business coach who could help them develop skills that would enhance their practice in this respect.

Assessment note: Assessors may only examine personnel records with the express consent of the relevant member of personnel. Records will be examined for their compliance with the practice's policy.

4.9 Practices *must* have a whistleblowing *policy*.

The whistleblowing policy should set out the types of issues that should be reported, what is unacceptable in respect thereto and to whom any such concerns should be reported. In addition, the policy should set out whether personnel should initially contact their line manager and to whom they should report the matter if it relates to their line manager.

The person that is notified of the issue should make it clear that the whistleblower can request that his or her concerns and allegations are treated in confidence and that he or she will not be penalised for taking steps to notify senior staff of concerns.

The policy should make reference to key legislation such as the Public Interest Disclosure Act (PIDA) 1998 which applies to the majority of workers and employees in Great Britain. There has been subsequent legislation such as the Enterprise and Regulatory Reform Act 2013, which addresses the circumstances that give rise to criminal offences, risks to health and safety and failures of a practice to meet legal obligations or miscarriages of justice and environmental damage.

It is also good practice to include information about the public interest test which was introduced by the government on 25 June 2013, which gives whistleblowers legal protection provided that certain procedures have been followed.

Sole practitioners: Sole practitioners that do not have any personnel do not need to document a whistleblowing policy.

4.10 Practices *must* have a *flexible working policy*.

Practices must take steps to ensure that the flexible working policy adheres to current legislation.

Issues that should be addressed as part of the policy include the following:

- Flexibility as to where personnel are based.
- When and at what times personnel work.
- The total number of hours that personnel work.

For example, working times, working locations or the pattern of work may be varied.

The flexible working policy should also set out whether the arrangements are formal or informal.

The flexible working policy should clearly set out a fair and accessible process for personnel to request an alternative working practice and how such requests are to be considered. The policy should support individuals to develop their full professional potential, regardless of working patterns.

It is good practice for the policy to define the various types of flexible working arrangements that practices will consider, for example compressed hours, part-time working, job sharing, remote working or flexible start and finish times.

It is considered good practice to include flexible working request forms and impact assessment forms to be completed by personnel when requesting a flexible working arrangement.

Practices are encouraged to be innovative and to harness technology and management skills to ensure flexible working arrangements are effective for all stakeholders, including the practice, its clients and personnel.

A review of the policy must take place at least annually. Issues to be considered include changes in legislation (although this should also be considered throughout the year), whether the policy is effective, technological advancements and any lessons learned from the previous 12 months that could improve the policy.

For more information on flexible working please see the Law Society's practice note on flexible working, which can be found at **www.lawsociety.org.uk/advice/practice-notes/flexible-working**.

Sole practitioners: Sole practitioners who employ any personnel, such as support staff, must ensure that their practice has a flexible working policy.

Large practices: Practices should actively communicate their flexible working policy to their personnel and have a mechanism for reviewing the effectiveness of the policy.

Assessment note: The flexible working policy may form part of the equality and diversity policy or be a standalone policy. Assessors will gather interview evidence and review the policy. With express permission of the relevant personnel, assessors may also access records of requests for flexible working, impact assessments and other job documentation, which may contribute to the overall level of compliance of the policy with the requirements at 4.10.

5 RISK MANAGEMENT

5.1 Practices *must* have a risk management *policy*, which *must* include:

(a) a compliance *plan*
(b) a *risk register*
(c) defined risk management roles and responsibilities
(d) arrangements for communicating risk information.

Risk is often defined as the likelihood and impact of an event. Practices are free to define risk in the context of their practice. The next step is to consider what a practice is trying to achieve by having a risk management policy and communicate this to personnel, as personnel need to understand the behaviours required of them. The risk management policy will need to be tailored to a practice's profile and tolerance to risk. Ideally, practices should undertake an analysis of risk issues from a strategic, operational and compliance perspective.

A compliance plan should set out the ways in which practices will comply with their regulatory obligations in respect of, for example:

- the SRA;
- health and safety;
- anti-money laundering;
- anti-bribery; and
- data protection.

The risk register often divides risks into the following categories:

- Strategic.
- Financial.
- Operational.
- Compliance.
- Breaches (material and non-material).

The register collates the risks. It may be held electronically or in hard copy.

Practices may wish to set out the risk management roles and responsibilities in the risk management policy or as part of the management structure that is required under 1.1(b). In the latter case it is not necessary to repeat this information in the risk policy, unless this will benefit the practice.

Sole practitioners: Sole practitioners that do not have any personnel can disregard 5.1(c) and (d).

Small and medium practices: For small and medium sized practices, some risk management roles and responsibilities may be delegated and this should be set out in the risk management policy or as part of the management structure that is required under 1.1(b).

There may also be a greater likelihood that external assistance will be required to meet some of the risk management responsibilities, as there may not be dedicated resources to deal with particular issues, for example, health and safety. If it is necessary to outsource particular activities then a practice should ensure there is no conflict between the risk management policy and the outsourcing policy at 5.2.

Arrangements for the communication of risk information may be informal but records should be kept of key issues, regardless of how small the practice is.

Large practices: The compliance plan is likely to be a fairly complex document.

The policy, particularly in relation to 5.1(c), should include how responsibilities are delegated on a day-to-day basis and whether any committees are convened to help effectively manage risk. A practice may have already included this information in an alternative location to comply with 1.1(b).

Communication arrangements should include both upward and downward communication, the form that communications should take and whether the communication should be documented or take the form of face-to-face discussions, or both. In large practices face-to-face meetings should be minuted to ensure accountability and that issues do not fall through the compliance 'net'.

Assessment note: Assessors will seek to verify that the documented policy is consistent with interview evidence. In particular, assessors will seek confirmation that the arrangements to communicate risk information are effective. The compliance plan and risk register may form part of the risk policy or be separate documents. Assessors will accept the method by which practices choose to organise their documents. In whatever manner the documents are organised, assessors will need to verify that the compliance plan and risk register exist. Assessors are likely to ask members of personnel questions in order to evaluate their understanding of the role the compliance plan and risk register play in managing risk.

5.2 Practices *must* have a *policy* in relation to outsourced activities, which *must* include:

(a) details of all outsourced activities including providers
(b) *procedures* to check the quality of outsourced work
(c) *procedures* to ensure providers have taken appropriate precautions to ensure information will be protected.

In order to comply with 5.2(a), practices may wish to keep a register of all the information on outsourced activities. As this relates to SRA compliance, practices may wish to include the register as part of the compliance plan.

If a practice is required to sign a provider's terms and conditions it should ensure that 5.2(c) is addressed in such terms and conditions or a practice must require the provider, separately, to take appropriate steps to safeguard information. The practice may wish to address 5.2(c) in its information management and security policy.

5.3 There *must* be a named *supervisor* for each area of work undertaken by the practice.

It is acceptable to make reference to roles rather than to name individuals, provided that those being supervised are aware of by whom they are being supervised. This information may already be set out in the management structure required by 1.1(b).

Sole practitioners: It is not necessary to document the information required in 5.3.

5.4 Practices *must* have *procedures* to manage instructions, which may be undertaken even though they have a higher *risk profile*, including unusual supervisory and reporting requirements or contingency planning.

The procedures must set out the types of matters that practices typically define as high risk and also have specific procedures to mitigate the risk, for example by having more frequent reviews of the matter file with a supervisor. The method by which practices manage each high risk matter is likely to vary, depending on the reasons why it was deemed to be high risk. This means that it is acceptable to set out specific procedures to manage risk on a case-by-case basis. This information should be apparent on the matter file to anyone who may undertake work on the file.

Sole practitioners: Sole practitioners do not need to document the procedures in place to manage matters which have a higher risk profile than usual. However, sole practitioners should be able to discuss with their assessor how high risk matters are managed and it must be made apparent in a matter file if the risk profile is high risk.

5.5 Practices *must* maintain lists of work that the practice will and will not undertake. This information *must* be communicated to all relevant *personnel* and *must* be updated when changes occur.

It is acceptable for practices to state the areas of work that they will undertake and then to state that they do not undertake any other areas of work.

It is also acceptable to capture this information on a practice's website, if it has one. However, practices should also ensure that this information is communicated to relevant personnel within the practice.

Sole practitioners: It is not necessary for sole practitioners to document the work that they will and will not undertake. However, it may be beneficial for practices to communicate this information externally and therefore practices may choose to document the work that they do undertake.

Large practices: It is considered good practice to communicate this information to new personnel during the induction process.

For existing personnel, a range of communication channels should be used to ensure that everyone understands the boundaries that they must work within. For example, practices may notify personnel of this information through a staff update and then reinforce this information through team meetings. It is considered good practice to have systems in place to monitor whether anyone within a practice deviates from the prescribed lists of work that the practice undertakes. Such systems should include even the most senior fee earners.

5.6 Practices *must* maintain details of the generic risks and causes of claims associated with the area(s) of work undertaken by the practice. This information *must* be communicated to all relevant *personnel*.

Each area of law presents different risks, which change over time. It is often helpful to draw upon fee earners' experiences and perceptions of what can cause claims in their area(s) of work, when practices are formulating the list of risks. In addition, insurers can often advise practices on trends in respect of claims across different areas of law. It is good practice to review these lists on a regular basis to ensure that the information contained therein is up to date.

Sole practitioners: As risks change over time, it is important for sole practitioners to update their knowledge of the risks that are relevant to the area(s) of law that they practise in. This will assist sole practitioners in maintaining details of generic risk and causes of claims in their practice area(s).

5.7 Practices *must* have a *procedure* to monitor key dates, which *must* include:

- **(a) the definition of key dates by work type**
- **(b) ensuring that key dates are recorded on the file and in a back-up system.**

Missing key dates gives rise to a significant number of negligence claims each year. The system that a practice adopts must ensure that the key dates are highly visible to the person with conduct of a matter, and also to any others who may need to deal with a matter in the absence of the fee earner with conduct.

Where a matter file is solely electronic, it may be acceptable to meet the requirements in 5.7 by having electronic alerts to help monitor key dates.

It is acceptable for the back-up system to be an electronic back-up, for example, where the case management system is backed up at the end of each day.

> **Assessment note:** Assessors will check key dates on matter files and how they are backed up. Interview evidence will assist assessors in understanding how they are monitored, so as not to be missed.

5.8 Practices *must* have a *policy* on the handling of conflicts, which *must* include:

- **(a) the definition of conflicts**
- **(b) training for all relevant *personnel* to identify conflicts**
- **(c) steps to be followed when a conflict is identified.**

The policy should encompass client and own interest conflicts.

The policy should also emphasise that fee earners are responsible for ensuring that there is no conflict of interest on their matters, even if certain aspects of the conflict check are performed by support personnel. Instigating and checking the results of a conflict check should always be within the remit of the fee earner.

If support personnel assist in performing the conflict of interest check, a practice must take steps to ensure that they are trained to an appropriate level. Fee earners should also receive appropriate training.

Fee earners should be aware that a conflict of interest may arise at any time during the course of a matter and so they must treat the conflict check not as a one-off check that is solely undertaken at the outset of a matter, but rather as an issue to be considered as a matter progresses as well.

> **Sole practitioners:** Sole practitioners should have a systematic method of checking for conflicts of interest. It is not acceptable to rely purely on memory to undertake a conflict check. A simple spreadsheet or database to check against would suffice should practices not have a case management system.

Assessment note: The assessor will gather evidence from matter files, as well as from interviews, to verify that the policy is working effectively.

5.9 Practices *must* have a *procedure* to ensure that all *personnel*, both permanent and temporary, are actively supervised. Such *procedures must* include:

(a) checks on incoming and outgoing correspondence where appropriate
(b) departmental, team and office meetings and communication structures
(c) reviews of matter details in order to ensure good financial controls and the appropriate allocation of workloads
(d) the exercise of devolved powers in publicly funded work
(e) the availability of a *supervisor*
(f) allocation of new work and reallocation of existing work, if necessary.

Regular supervision helps practices to control the implementation and use of their policies and procedures. When carried out effectively, this can create significant benefits, ensuring that practices manage risk effectively. In addition, practices may often find that such processes can assist them in identifying areas where personnel require development (such as training) or other issues relating to personnel.

Practices should be aware that the onus is on the supervisor to be available and actively supervising personnel. This includes ensuring that those under supervision have a manageable workload and are carrying out work that is at an appropriate level commensurate with their qualification and experience.

Supervising e-mails can be challenging, particularly due to the increasing volume of electronic communication and document formats. Practices may supervise e-mails in a variety of ways. For example, an e-mail could be printed off and put in the matter file.

Practices may have a policy that defines which e-mails must be reviewed before they are sent and which are not subject to prior supervision. This may be done by assigning risk categories to different types of e-mails.

As part of 5.9(b), practices should also consider whether it is appropriate for support personnel to attend team or departmental meetings, dependent upon how closely they work with fee earners.

The implication of 5.9(c) is that there must be some form of financial review. This may be most effectively undertaken as part of the independent file reviews that are required to be undertaken at 5.11.

Sole practitioners: Sole practitioners that do not have any personnel do not need to document their procedures for supervision. However, if sole practitioners intend to employ locums or temporary fee earners to assist them then some form of supervision is necessary and should be documented.

Large practices: In large practices the greatest challenge in relation to supervision can be having effective channels of communication, particularly if there are teams or departments that are based in different locations. Practices should define the frequency and the format of the meetings required at 5.9(b). Unless there is a very good reason for not having office meetings, they should take place at least annually. Team and departmental meetings typically take place monthly, bi-monthly or quarterly, depending on the work area and the experience of the personnel.

5.10 Practices *must* have a *procedure* to ensure that all those doing legal work check their files regularly for inactivity.

There are two main methods of checking files for inactivity. If the files are in hard copy, practices may conduct a 'cabinet trawl' on a regular basis. However, if there is a case management system or the ability to time record electronically, fee earners can usually check when files were last worked on.

The focus of this requirement is for fee earners with conduct of a matter to check their files for inactivity. However, checking for inactivity can also be a useful supervision tool and supervisors may wish to review inactive file lists with fee earners as part of supervision meetings.

It should be noted that it is acceptable for matters to be inactive if there is a valid reason for such inactivity, for example, waiting for the other side to respond within a certain time period. However, the purpose of 5.10 is to avoid inadvertently failing to progress a matter.

5.11 Practices *must* have a *procedure* for regular, independent file reviews of either the management of the file or its substantive legal content, or both. In relation to file reviews, practices *must*:

(a) define and explain file selection criteria
(b) define and explain the number and frequency of reviews
(c) retain a record of the file review on the matter file and centrally
(d) ensure any corrective action which is identified in a file review is acted upon within 28 days and verified
(e) ensure that the designated *supervisor* reviews and monitors the data generated by file reviews
(f) conduct a review at least annually of the data generated by file reviews.

The file selection criteria should set out the reasoning behind why and how files are selected for review. When defining the file selection criteria it is appropriate to consider the following:

- How to select a representative sample of the fee earner's files.
- Whether files should be selected randomly.
- If the fee earner is managing high risk matters, whether those files should be reviewed more frequently.
- Whether to select files based on activity or lack of activity.
- Whether files which are at different stages of completion should be selected.

File reviews, although they often will be, do not have to be undertaken by the designated supervisor in person, for example, reviews are sometimes outsourced. Where supervisors do not undertake the file reviews in person it will need to be apparent that they will be made aware of the outcome of the file reviews. It is important also that fee earners are involved in the file review arrangements, including partners and senior managers. The frequency and depth of reviews often reflect the seniority and experience of the person having conduct of a matter.

Ideally, file reviews are undertaken by someone other than the person with conduct of the matter. However, in sole practices and where there is only one fee earner practising in an area of law, it may not be possible to identify anyone else who could comment on legal issues. Where this is the case, a supervisor, a fee earner in another category, a suitably trained manager or an administrator may carry out the file review of the management of the file and this must be reflected in the practice's policy. If a sole practitioner is the only fee earner, the process of case management and client care activity can be reviewed by a member of personnel.

Another option is that file reviews could be outsourced, for example, where there are reciprocal arrangements with fellow local sole practitioners. It will be important to ensure that client confidentiality is controlled in such cases, however, and that no conflicts of interests arise from the operation of such arrangements.

The review will generally embrace technical and procedural issues but it is ultimately for the practice to decide. A decision not to embrace technical and procedural issues is more likely for sole practitioners or in very small practices where there is no prospect of another person within the practice having the necessary expertise to assess the technical content of the file.

File reviews will also highlight corrective action that is needed and record when it has been completed. The mechanism for the corrective action is for the practice to decide. However, it should be borne in mind that the corrective action must take place within a maximum of 28 days.

In respect of 5.11(c), the requirement is not that the full review be held on the matter file, but rather that it be apparent from the file that it has been reviewed and where the central record of such review may be found. It is increasingly common to have a central record of file reviews which is in an electronic format. This will be compliant, provided that it is apparent from the matter file that it has been subject to a file review and that the outcome of the file review can be easily traced.

There is no minimum requirement in relation to how many file reviews should be undertaken. However, practices need to ensure that they have sufficient information to identify trends when they undertake the annual review of data, required by 5.11(f).

5.12 Operational risk *must* be considered and recorded in all matters before, during and after the processing of instructions. Before the matter is undertaken, the fee earners *must*:

(a) consider if a new client and/or matter is accepted by the practice, in accordance with section 6.1 and 6.7 below
(b) assess the risk profile of all new instructions and notify the *supervisor*, in accordance with *procedures* under 5.4, of any unusual or high risk considerations in order that appropriate action may be taken.

During the retainer the fee earner *must*:

(c) consider any change to the *risk profile* of the matter and report and advise on such circumstances without delay, informing the *supervisor* if appropriate
(d) inform the client in all cases where an adverse costs order is made against the practice in relation to the matter in question.

At the end of the matter the fee earner *must*:

(e) undertake a concluding risk assessment by considering if the client's *objectives* have been achieved
(f) notify the *supervisor* of all such circumstances in accordance with documented *procedures* in section 5.4 above.

The essence of 5.12 is that risk needs to be considered and recorded before, during and after the work is performed for the client. Fee earners should be aware of risk issues over the full duration of a matter.

The risk assessment must be recorded at the outset and at the end of each matter. During the matter, however, the risk assessment should only be recorded if the risk level has changed from the initial level.

An initial risk assessment should be based on the instructions received and must be recorded. The identification of any special or high risk issues will then need to be referred to the relevant supervisor via a procedure established for doing so. This could be either a risk notice or a section in the matter opening form highlighting 'high' or 'unusual' risk associated with the instructions or the client or an entry in the risk register.

The ongoing risk profile should be considered during the entire course of the retainer. If the risk to the client or the firm changes materially, for example, if third parties are joined in litigation, materially adding to costs risks, or counsel's opinion is obtained, casting doubt on advice already provided to the client, then the client will need to be informed and consulted without delay. Adverse costs orders need to be reported immediately as they will usually have to be paid forthwith. There is no particular point in the course of a matter at which the fee earner should undertake an ongoing risk assessment, but the fee earner should be aware of changes in risk throughout the life of the matter.

The purpose of the concluding risk assessment should be to consider the following:

- Whether the client's objectives have been met.
- Whether the client is likely to complain.
- Whether the fee earner is aware of any circumstances that may give rise to a negligence claim that have not already been notified to his or her supervisor.

A closing risk assessment should always be recorded on the matter file.

> **Sole practitioners:** Sole practitioners need to ensure that they are considering and recording levels of risk associated with new clients and instructions. However, they do not need to set out reporting arrangements as they are self-supervising.

5.13 Practices *must* have a *policy* to ensure compliance with anti-money laundering legislation, which *must* include:

(a) the appointment of a nominated officer usually referred to as a Money Laundering Reporting Officer (MLRO)
(b) a *procedure* for making disclosures within the practice and by the MLRO to the authorities
(c) *procedures* for checking the identity of the practice's clients
(d) a *plan* for the training of *personnel*
(e) *procedures* for the proper maintenance of records.

The Law Society has produced a comprehensive practice note on anti-money laundering. For guidance on this topic please visit **www.lawsociety.org.uk/advice/practice-notes/aml**.

> **Assessment note:** An assessor's role is not to audit practices against legislation but to assess them against their own policy. Assessors should take steps, however, to familiarise themselves with the current regulations to enable them to identify that all key issues are included in the policy. File reviews will provide evidence of compliance with the policy, for example, records of identity checks that may be retained on the matter file.

5.14 Practices *should* have a *policy* in relation to the avoidance of involvement in property and mortgage fraud, which *must* include:

(a) carrying out relevant checks in relation to the conveyancer acting for the other party.

Practices that do not undertake property work do not need to have a policy in relation to 5.14.

The policy should set out the typical warning signs of potential mortgage fraud and who to contact if fee earners have any concerns. This policy should be kept under regular review as criminals frequently change tactics in an attempt to commit mortgage fraud. Regular communication and training in this area are critical to the success of the policy.

Practices may also wish to refer to the Law Society's practice note on mortgage fraud, to help formulate the practice's policy. Please see **www.lawsociety.org.uk/advice/practice-notes/mortgage-fraud**.

> **Assessment note:** This is an optional requirement. An assessor will seek interview evidence and review matter files to verify that the documented policy is working effectively.

5.15 Practices *must* have a *policy* setting out the *procedures* to prevent bribery in accordance with current legislation.

The policy should set out the purpose of the policy and establish boundaries for all personnel to work within. A register that records gifts and hospitality should assist with the internal controls used to monitor that the policy is being adhered to and is effective.

Practices must ensure that the policy addresses current legal obligations. For further information please see the Law Society's anti-bribery practice note at **www.lawsociety.org.uk/advice/practice-notes/bribery-act-2010**.

> **Assessment note:** Assessors should familiarise themselves with anti-bribery legislation. However, an assessor is verifying that a practice has implemented its policy, not assessing a practice's interpretation of the legislation. Assessors may find it useful to access the gift register, if one exists.

5.16 Practices will analyse at least annually all risk assessment data generated within the practice. This *must* include:

(a) any indemnity insurance claims (where applicable)
(b) an analysis of client complaints trends
(c) data generated by file reviews
(d) any matters notified to the COLP and/or COFA
(e) any material breaches notified to the SRA
(f) any non-material breaches recorded
(g) situations where the practice acted where a conflict existed
(h) the identification of remedial action.

The purpose of the annual review is to identify ways in which practices can improve their risk profile. Therefore, it is useful to draw together as much information as possible to enable practices to understand their current risk profile and any remedial action that may be necessary. By compiling all of the information set out in this requirement, practices should be able to identify trends across their practice and to take appropriate steps to improve their risk profile.

The SRA states that:

> the COLP and COFA should be champions of risk management and compliance within a firm, and will have responsibility for the firm's systems and controls. They are responsible for ensuring processes are in place to enable the firm, its managers and employees and anyone who has any interest in the firm to comply with Handbook requirements on them.

Therefore, the COLP and COFA roles are vital to Lexcel compliance as Lexcel provides a robust framework to deal with risk issues. 5.16(d) requires that issues that have been notified to the COLP and COFA over the preceding 12 months form part of the annual review of risk.

Practices may also consider including client feedback in the annual analysis of risk assessment data, as this can provide additional insight into the client experience and possibly whether there are likely to be any future complaints or claims.

Large practices: There may be a significant amount of risk information to manage across a large practice. As such, it may be most effective for larger practices to undertake a quarterly or six-monthly review.

Assessment note: Assessors will need sight of the annual review and will seek evidence that any remedial action has been carried out or is scheduled to take place.

6 CLIENT CARE

6.1 Practices *must* have a *policy* for client care, including:

- **(a) how enquiries from potential clients will be dealt with**
- **(b) ensuring that before taking on a client, the practice has sufficient resources and competence to deal with the matter**
- **(c) protecting client confidentiality**
- **(d) a timely response is made to telephone calls and correspondence from the client and others**
- **(e) a *procedure* for referring clients to third parties**
- **(f) the provision of *reasonable adjustments* for disabled clients.**

Practices must consider the key issues that will ensure the effective delivery of their services and record their commitment in this regard in a client care policy. It will be for each practice to determine its approach to the style and format of documentation and, in particular, whether it forms part of a more general policy document or is produced separately.

The policy should include information in relation to:

- responsibility for client care;
- general approach of the practice;
- actions that will be taken to test and improve client care; and
- specific behaviours expected from personnel when dealing with clients.

In relation to 6.1(f), practices must comply with their obligations to ensure reasonable adjustments are made for disabled clients and personnel. The duty to make reasonable adjustments applies to the provision of services in the same way as it applies in an employer–employee situation.

There is no set formula to determine whether an adjustment is reasonable. In the majority of cases, the provider of the services will be expected to make every effort to accommodate the needs of those with a disability.

When practices consider reasonable adjustments, they must give careful consideration as to whether a disabled client will be at a 'substantial disadvantage', if the adjustment is not made. This term is defined in the current legislation as being 'more than minor or trivial'.

In addition to this, outcome 2.3 of the SRA Code of Conduct requires practices to make adjustments for disabled clients without passing on the cost of such adjustments to the client.

In some circumstances it may be useful to obtain advice from expert disability organisations who can assist with guidance, signposting and other forms of support.

The Law Society has produced a practice note that provides additional guidance. The practice note can be found at **www.lawsociety.org.uk/advice/practice-notes/equality-and-diversity-requirements--sra-handbook.**

Assessment note: Assessors will compare the documented policy with interview evidence from personnel. Assessors need to understand how work is allocated in order to assess compliance against 6.1(b). Assessors may also seek evidence on matter files as to how the policy is working in practice, for example, in relation to responding in a timely manner to clients and others. Matter files may provide an assessor with evidence that reasonable adjustments have been made, such as file notes to confirm that home visits have been made to clients or correspondence in large print.

6.2 Practices *must* communicate the following to clients in writing, unless an alternative form of communication is deemed more appropriate:

- **(a) where appropriate, establish the client's requirements and *objectives***
- **(b) provide a clear explanation of the issues involved and the options available to the client**
- **(c) explain what the fee earner will and will not do**
- **(d) agree with the client the next steps to be taken**
- **(e) keep the client informed of progress, as agreed**
- **(f) establish in what timescale that matter will be dealt with**
- **(g) establish the method of funding**
- **(h) where appropriate, consider whether the intended action would be merited on a cost benefit analysis**
- **(i) agree an appropriate level of service**
- **(j) explain the practice's responsibilities and the client's**
- **(k) provide the client with the name and status of the person dealing with their matter**
- **(l) provide the client with the name and status of the person responsible for the overall supervision of their matter.**

The information referred to at 6.2(a)–(l), in essence, forms the basis of the client care letter or terms of business. The fee earner must ensure that due regard is given to the SRA Handbook, particularly Chapter 1 of the Code of Conduct. The Law Society's practice note can be found at **www.lawsociety.org.uk/advice/practice-notes/client-care-letters**.

Assessment note: Assessors will seek evidence from the matter file that the client has been provided with all the information set out in 6.2. There may be circumstances where it is not appropriate to send the client correspondence setting out this information. Assessors will seek evidence that the client has been provided with the information and that a record is on the file by way of an attendance note.

6.3 Practices *must* have a record of any standing terms of business with regular clients. The practice *must* be able to produce such terms in relation to issues covered by this section.

Before agreeing to offer standing terms of business to a regular client, it is necessary to differentiate between those clients that instruct the practice repeatedly in relation to similar matters and those that instruct the practice repeatedly but in relation to different matters.

It is unlikely that practices could have standing terms of business with a client where the matters they have asked the practice to deal with span across a range of legal areas, for example, being instructed in relation to the purchase of a house and then the sale of a commercial property. However, if practices were instructed by a client to deal with several similar debt collection matters, it would probably be appropriate to have standing terms of business with that client.

> **Assessment note:** Assessors must satisfy themselves that the standard terms of business have been communicated to the client and cover the work being undertaken in all matters. The matter file as well as the standard terms will provide evidence to verify this.

6.4 Practices *must* give clients the best information possible about the likely overall cost of the matter, both at the outset and when appropriate, as the matter progresses. In particular practices *must*:

(a) advise the client of the basis of the practice's charging
(b) advise the client where the practice will receive a financial benefit as a result of accepting instructions
(c) advise the client if the charging rates are to be increased
(d) advise the client of likely payments which the practice or the client may need to make to others
(e) discuss with the client how they will pay
(f) advise the client that there are circumstances where the practice may be entitled to exercise a lien for unpaid costs
(g) advise the client of their potential liability for any other party's costs.

Fee earners should have received training so that they understand the information that their practice is required to provide the client with in relation to 6.4.

Much of this information is typically included in the client care letter or terms of business provided to the client at the outset of the matter. However, practices should ensure that any changes are communicated to the client as the matter progresses.

Again, as with 6.2, practices must ensure that they are compliant with the SRA Handbook, particularly in relation to Chapter 1 of the Code of Conduct.

Assessment note: This information must be documented on the matter file, usually by way of correspondence to the client. However, there may be circumstances where an attendance note is adequate to evidence communication of this information to the client.

6.5 Practices *must* operate a written complaints handling *procedure*, including:

(a) the definition of what the practice regards as a complaint
(b) informing the client at the outset of the matter, that in the event of a problem they are entitled to complain
(c) the name of the person with overall responsibility for complaints
(d) providing the client with a copy of the practice's complaints *procedure*, if requested
(e) once a complaint has been made, the person complaining is informed in writing:
(i) how the complaint will be handled; and
(ii) in what time they will be given an initial and/or substantive response
(f) recording and reporting centrally all complaints received from clients
(g) identifying the cause of any problems of which the client has complained offering any appropriate redress, and correcting any unsatisfactory *procedures*.

The Legal Ombudsman's website contains a large amount of information that should assist practices in formulating their complaints handling procedure.

For more information, please visit **www.legalombudsman.org.uk**.

Practices should ideally review the analysis of complaints, as this will indicate the areas in which they are most at risk of receiving a complaint and where additional training or other support may be required.

Sole practitioners: Sole practitioners may find it challenging to deal with complaints where they are the only fee earner within the practice, as they will be dealing with complaints about an aspect of the service that they have provided themselves. Sole practitioners may wish to contact an external organisation that could potentially assist them in dealing independently with complaints, for example, some local law societies offer this service.

Assessment note: Assessors will seek evidence from matter files that clients have been provided with the appropriate information in relation to complaints, in accordance with a practice's procedure. Assessors will verify that the Legal Ombudsman information is included in a practice's procedures. The central register of complaints will need to be reviewed to verify that complaints are being dealt with in accordance with the procedures. Interview evidence will be gathered to help assessors understand whether the documented complaints procedures are working effectively.

6.6 Practices *must* have a *procedure* to monitor client satisfaction across all areas of the practice.

A practice's procedures need to set out the steps to be followed to gather client feedback across all areas of work it undertakes. There is no single method prescribed by Lexcel to monitor client satisfaction. Practices will need to have regard to the profile of their clients and decide on the most appropriate method of monitoring client satisfaction. Practices may choose to monitor client feedback differently, by work type, for example, by way of a questionnaire in the conveyancing department and face-to-face meetings with corporate clients. Practices do not have to monitor the satisfaction of all clients but may do so on a sample basis.

> **Assessment note:** Assessors will verify that the procedures are in operation by comparing the documentation against interview evidence. Assessors should seek to understand how practices manage the data produced by the procedures.

6.7 Practices *must* have a *procedure* to accept or decline instructions, which *must* include:

(a) how decisions are made to accept instructions from new and existing clients
(b) how decisions are made to stop acting for an existing client
(c) how decisions are made to decline instructions.

When drafting the procedures in relation to 6.7, practices should take steps to align the client care policy and their strategy with their requirements. The risk policy and supervisory arrangements should also align with their procedures. Practices should include information in the terms of business that explain to clients the circumstances in which they may stop acting.

> **Assessment note:** Assessors will verify the procedures are in operation by gathering interview evidence. The risk register and matter files may also reveal details as to how the procedures are operating.

7 FILE AND CASE MANAGEMENT

7.1 Practices *must* ensure that the strategy for a matter is always apparent on the matter file and that in complex cases a project plan is developed.

All matters must have a clear strategy which is apparent on the matter file.

The information that is recorded on the matter file, which is a requirement of 6.2, 7.3 and 7.4, will usually reveal the strategy of a matter. However, if a matter is complex then a separate project plan is required. Essentially, the information held on the matter file, whether hard copy or electronic copy should tell the whole story of the file, including the strategy.

This requirement forms part of the risk management framework within Lexcel. Fulfilling this requirement will help to ensure that if there is a complaint or potential claim, the file can easily be reviewed by someone other than the fee earner and that such person would have a clear understanding of the strategy for the matter and whether the fee earner has discharged his or her duty.

It is for practices to define what a complex matter/case is. However, practices may wish to consider the following issues when deciding whether to create a complex case plan:

- Whether it is subject to High Court jurisdiction.
- The level of costs or potential costs.
- Whether it is or is likely to be a multi-party action.

Sole practitioners: Even though sole practitioners may be the only fee earner in their practice, it is crucial to ensure that each matter file contains a record of all the relevant information.

There may be occasions when those that are external to the practice, such as insurers or regulators, will need to review a file and understand the strategy of the matter and what has taken place without the opportunity to seek further information from the sole practitioner.

Large practices: It is for practices to define what constitutes a complex matter. However, if the matter involves multiple areas of law, it would be usual to expect a project plan to exist in order to help co-ordinate the various activities required to meet the client's objectives.

Assessment note: The file or case plan should be capable of being read and understood independently of the fee earner with conduct of the matter and the assessor should be able to understand the strategy of the matter.

7.2 Practices *must* document *procedures* for the giving, monitoring and discharge of undertakings.

Failure to honour an undertaking is on the face of it professional misconduct. This could be dealt with at a disciplinary tribunal and is enforceable by the courts through their inherent jurisdiction.

The procedures should address who within a practice is permitted to give undertakings and the consequences for personnel, should they be found to be in breach of the procedures.

Practices may decide to subdivide the procedure for undertakings by department, as the type and frequency of undertakings can significantly vary by work type.

Given the potential damage that could be suffered, practices will wish to consider how and when undertakings should be provided. Common arrangements will be to distinguish routine and non-routine undertakings and apply different safeguards to them. Conveyancing departments are likely to specify who can provide routine undertakings on exchange and completion of contracts. Consideration should be given to the procedure for authorising undertakings required by a court as practicalities may require special arrangements.

There is no requirement for a central register of undertakings, though some practices find this helpful and it is considered good practice. Practices may use software, such as a case management system or spreadsheet to centralise undertaking records into a register. This may assist practices in monitoring undertakings.

> **Assessment note:** Assessors will need to gather evidence from the matter files and any central register of undertakings, if one exists, to confirm whether this requirement has been met.

7.3 Practices *must* have a *procedure* to:

- **(a) list open and closed matters, identify all matters for a single client and linked files where relevant and all files for a particular funder**
- **(b) ensure that they are able to identify and trace any documents, files, deeds, wills or any other items relating to the matter**
- **(c) safeguard the confidentiality of matter files and all other client information**
- **(d) ensure that the status of the matter and the action taken can be easily checked by other members of the practice**
- **(e) ensure that documents are stored on the matter file(s) in an orderly way.**

Most practices will be able to identify the funders of matters (e.g. the Legal Aid Agency, named trade unions or legal expense insurers) through a computer coding system.

Practices that have a case management system should find it relatively easy to comply with 7.3. However, those practices that do not have such a system will need to devise a method of complying with 7.3(a), for example, by managing the information on a spreadsheet or database.

Practices should ensure that their information management and security policy is consistent with their procedures under 7.3(c).

Conveyancing departments should be able to link sale and purchase files for the same client in linked transactions.

As a general rule all records relating to a matter should be capable of being traced by being either on the file itself or referred to thereon. When a file is contained in a number of folders or lever arch files, there should be some method by which they can be shown to belong to the same matter. This could be achieved by the use of the client/matter reference number and an indication on each part, e.g. '1 of 2'; '2 of 2', etc. or 'Correspondence from 01.01.14 to 09.09.14', or by listing on a schedule, kept in a prominent part of the file. Where there are ancillary papers or other records (e.g. x-rays or medical records in clinical negligence work) they should be linked to the file in question by tagging or use of the client/matter numbering system.

Consideration should be given to all the circumstances where safeguarding the confidentiality of the client could be at risk (e.g. files being worked on during a train journey, files left in unattended cars, etc.). Where clients are seen in the reception area there should be arrangements for consultations, even if very short, to be conducted out of earshot of other clients or visitors in the reception area. The requirements in 7.3(c) should align with the requirements in 3.1 relating to information management and security.

The state of matter files is an important consideration under this section. Showing key information on a file summary sheet or colour-coding of notes of meetings, reviews or letters to the client are helpful options.

Assessment note: Where computer case management systems are used, assessors will need to check the protocols for naming and storing documents and for making regular back-ups. Assessors should follow audit trails to ensure that key documents can be located where they are not stored on the matter file.

7.4 Practices will have *procedures* to ensure that matters are progressed in an appropriate manner. In particular:

- **(a) key information *must* be recorded on the file**
- **(b) a timely response is made to telephone calls and correspondence from the client and others**
- **(c) continuing cost information is provided**
- **(d) clients are informed in writing if the person with conduct of their matter changes, or there is a change of person to whom any problem with service may be addressed.**

The requirements set out in 7.4 are closely aligned to those in section 6, which deals with client care, particularly the client care policy requirements in 6.1. Whether the practice has electronic or hard copy files, it must ensure that key information is recorded on the file. Key information includes:

- correspondence;
- attendance notes;
- records of conversations;
- evidence;
- draft wills; and
- deeds.

Practices must ensure that evidence and/or documents that are not held on the matter file are clearly traceable to the matter file, for example, where wills are stored in a strongroom or fireproof cabinet.

When deciding which information is key and should therefore be recorded on the matter file, it is considered best practice to record all telephone conversations as it is not always obvious at the time which of these may contain key information.

7.4(b) requires practices to have procedures to ensure that clients and others are responded to in a timely manner. Therefore, practices must set out what they consider to be timely and manage client expectations accordingly.

7.4(c) requires practices to provide continuing cost information to their clients. Practices must inform clients of all costs before they are incurred or additional work is undertaken. However, if the original costs estimate or fee quoted has not changed since the start of a matter, it is not necessary to provide an update on costs.

Practices should consider setting a regular timeframe within which updates must be provided. This could be monthly or every three or six months, depending on the type of matter. Alternatively, practices may have a finance team or an accounting system that can provide alerts as a cost limit approaches, which would enable practices to notify clients promptly of any likely changes to costs.

Sole practitioners: Sole practitioners do not need to document the procedures in relation to 7.4(d) as they are the only fee earner in their practice. However, sole practitioners who use locums to provide holiday cover will need to ensure that their clients are aware of who to contact in their absence.

Small and medium practices: It is considered best practice to ensure that a practice's file review system includes checking that fee earners are complying with the practice's procedures to meet this requirement. Failing to progress matters appropriately may indicate a problem, which could lead to a complaint or claim.

Large practices: It is considered best practice to ensure that a practice's file review system includes checking that fee earners are complying with the practice's procedures to meet this requirement. Failing to progress matters appropriately may indicate a problem, which could lead to a complaint or claim.

If the person responsible for handling complaints changes, it can be an onerous task to notify all clients. Consideration should be given as to the best way to communicate this information. For example, whether it would be appropriate to request that fee earners notify their clients of this change the next time that they correspond with them or whether practices simply forward any complaints for the previous complaints handler to the new complaints handler, who can then notify the client that he or she is dealing with the complaint.

Assessment note: Assessors should be able to get a complete picture of a matter by reviewing the key information on the matter file. If a file includes all key information, an assessor should not need to ask questions of the fee earner with conduct of the matter in order to understand the progress of the matter.

In assessing whether sufficient information has been given on the progress of matters and a timely response has been made to telephone calls or correspondence, assessors will take into account any instructions or preferences that the client has expressed in this regard. Where a firm stipulates response times (e.g. all telephone calls from clients to be returned within 24 hours) they will be assessed on this basis. Assessors will seek evidence of compliance both by checking the matter files and by interviewing members of personnel.

7.5 Practices *must* have a documented *procedure* for using barristers, expert witnesses and other external advisers who are involved in the delivery of legal services, which *must* include provision for the following:

(a) use of clear selection criteria in line with the equality and diversity *policy*
(b) where appropriate, consult with the client in relation to the selection of an advocate or other professional
(c) advising the client of the name and status of the person being instructed, how long she/he might take to respond and, where disbursements are to be paid by the client, the cost involved
(d) maintenance of records (centrally, by department or office) on barristers and experts used, including evidence of assessment against the criteria
(e) *evaluation* of performance, for the information of other members of the practice
(f) giving clear instructions
(g) checking of opinions and reports received to ensure they adequately provide the information sought (and, in litigation matters, comply with the rules of court and any court orders)
(h) payment of fees.

The selection criteria for experts and barristers must comply with the equality and diversity policy under 4.2. In addition, 7.5(b) states that where appropriate a client should be consulted on the choice. This is more likely to be appropriate in respect of commercial clients as they may well have a preference or they may wish to approve the choice of candidate.

Regardless of size, the most efficient and practical way to manage records relating to experts is by utilising a central register. This may be held in an electronic or hard copy form.

Practices may wish to include evidence of the selection criteria with the central records required by 7.5(d) or hold them separately.

It is acceptable to evaluate the performance of experts and barristers on a case-by-case basis and record this in an attendance note which is kept on the matter file. Alternatively, practices may centralise the records of performance evaluations of experts and barristers.

7.6 Practices *must* have *procedures* to ensure that, at the end of the matter, the practice:

- **(a) if required, reports to the client on the outcome and explains any further action that the client is required to take in the matter and what (if anything) the practice will do**
- **(b) accounts to the client for any outstanding money**
- **(c) returns to the client any original documents or other property belonging to the client if required (save for items which are by agreement to be stored by the practice)**
- **(d) if appropriate, advises the client about arrangements for storage and retrieval of papers and other items retained (in so far as this has not already been dealt with, for example in terms of business) and any charges to be made in this regard**
- **(e) advises the client whether it is appropriate to review the matter in future and, if so, when and why**
- **(f) archives and destroys files in an appropriate manner.**

It is essential that matter files are closed effectively. In most practices a reminder and checklist are provided which highlight the issues covered in this section. These can be found either on the file summary or in a file closing sheet. It would be unusual for practices not to report the outcome of the matter to the client.

7.6(b) may not always be relevant, but where it is, this should be completed promptly at the conclusion of the matter to ensure good financial management.

Practices should conduct a final risk assessment to consider if there are circumstances that should be reported to a supervisor or the COLP (see also 5.12). If a sole practitioner is the person responsible for risk management, a note of any such circumstances should still be made in relation to his or her own files as this information contributes to the annual review of risk (see also 5.16). In private practice, noting issues of concern at the end of a matter might necessitate a report to the practice's insurers.

Neither the Law Society nor the SRA advise on any particular period for the retention of files before they are destroyed, but practices should note that the Money Laundering Regulations 2007 (SI 2007/2157) require certain records to be kept for at least five years. The Legal Aid Agency stipulates as a term of its criminal and civil contracts that files must be retained for a fixed period after closure.

When files are being archived or destroyed, practices should give consideration to confidentiality, data protection and information management and security issues.

Practices should ensure that the requirements of 7.6(f) are consistent with their information management and security policy.

Assessment note: Assessors will select a sample of closed files to verify whether the procedures at 7.6 are being adhered to in practice.

PART II

The Standard for in-house legal departments

Introduction

WHO IS LEXCEL FOR?

- Legal departments in any jurisdiction in the world can apply for accreditation against the Lexcel Standard, regardless of the size or type of work undertaken. See the **Scheme rules** for further details.
- Two versions of Lexcel are available to reflect the needs of domestic and international markets:

  - **Lexcel England and Wales** – version 6 of the Standard for legal practices in England and Wales.
  - **Lexcel International** – version 5 of the Standard for practices in England and Wales with independent offices overseas and practices in foreign jurisdictions.

- Lexcel England and Wales is divided into two versions to meet the needs of legal practices and in-house legal departments. These entities are defined as:

  - **A law practice** in the form of partnerships, limited liability partnerships, sole practitioners, incorporated law firms and alternative business structures (ABSs) authorised and regulated by the Solicitors Regulation Authority (SRA).
  - **An in-house legal department**, including those in corporations, the public sector (including ABSs), law centres and not-for-profit and government organisations.

- For ease of reference, the generic term 'department' is used throughout the Standard. This refers to any in-house legal team or legal department that is part of a wider organisation.
- In-house legal departments with multiple offices can apply by jurisdiction. For example, an in-house legal department with five departments across England and Wales must submit one application and be assessed across all five departments. In contrast, one that has two departments in England and Wales and an independent department overseas would need to submit two applications, if they wanted to apply for Lexcel across multiple jurisdictions. It is not mandatory for all in-house legal departments across a range of jurisdictions to apply for Lexcel. Please see the **Scheme rules** for further details.
- Lexcel can be combined with other quality standards including ISO 9001, Investors in People and the Specialist Quality Mark (SQM) and could reduce the time and cost of assessment. A joint assessment may also be possible.
- Lexcel is accepted as a quality standard by the Legal Aid Agency, instead of accreditation against the SQM.
- An annual practice registration fee is payable to the Law Society and a fee is also payable to the independent assessment body.

- The annual in-house department registration fee is divided into five bands, based on the number of admitted and non-admitted legal advisors in the department:

  - 1 legal advisor
  - 2 – 15 legal advisors
  - 16 – 40 legal advisors
  - 41 – 85 legal advisors
  - 86+ legal advisors

GLOSSARY OF TERMS AND GUIDANCE

- **Emphasised words** (apart from document headings) in the Lexcel Standard are defined in the **Glossary of Terms**.
- A main requirement is presented as a numbered paragraph. Specific requirements are listed as subclauses.
- Separate **Guidance notes** provide further explanation of requirements and are divided into general and specific guidance based on whether or not the in-house legal department has external or internal clients.
- In-house legal departments have the flexibility to implement procedures that are appropriate to their circumstances in order to meet requirements in the Standard.
- Most in-house legal departments will document all procedures in an office manual, but there is no specific requirement that prevents procedures being documented in a number of different sources.
- Although Lexcel will help in-house legal departments and organisations comply with some aspects of legislation, accreditation does not guarantee compliance with local laws. This remains the responsibility of the organisation.

QUESTIONS?

If, after reading the Standard, **Scheme rules** and **Guidance notes**, you have any questions regarding Lexcel, please do not hesitate to contact us:

Tel: +44 (0)20 7320 5933
E-mail: lexcel@lawsociety.org.uk

The Lexcel Standard for in-house legal departments

GLOSSARY OF TERMS

Term	Definition
Authorisations	Organisations need to consider whether authorisation **procedures** need to be in place whereby different **personnel** are given permission to approve expenditure to pre-defined levels.
Corporate social responsibility (CSR)	For the purposes of Lexcel, **CSR** is defined as the commitment of an organisation or department to operate in an ethical manner and contribute in a positive way to society. This is an optional requirement for departments, although organisations tendering for the provision of legal services to other organisations may be required to have a **CSR policy** in place.
Evaluation	To make a judgement.
External client(s)	Clients that are not part of the organisation.
Flexible working	**Flexible working** practices have become increasingly relevant to the legal sector as part of recruitment and retention. Some examples of **flexible working** are part time working, annualised hours, compressed hours and remote working.
Malicious software (malware)	Software that is used to disrupt computer operation, gather sensitive data or gain access to private computer systems.
Must	A mandatory requirement.
Objective(s)	Any **objectives** agreed and set out need to be measurable. They will require some form of quantification or have indicators of progress to measure performance.
Personnel	All employed staff and locums.
Plan(s)	A '**plan**' is a documented outline of where an organisation or department desires to be in the future and describes how it intends to arrive at that destination. A **plan** can be described as a map which supports an organisation or a department to arrive at their desired destination in the future. In general, the Lexcel Standard permits organisations or the department to develop **plans** in the manner and detail that the organisation or department considers appropriate, assuming a basic level of adequacy. All **plans must** have a named person who is responsible for the **plan**. They **must** also be reviewed at least annually.
Policy/policies	A '**policy**' is a documented general approach taken within the organisation or department to the issue in question. A **policy** defines why a particular approach is adopted by the organisation or department. All **policies must** have a named person who is responsible for the **policy**. They **must** also be reviewed at least annually.

Procedure(s)	A '**procedure**' is a written description of how an activity will occur within the department or organisation. A **procedure** describes the steps that **personnel** are required to follow in order to complete an activity. At an assessment, a **procedure** can only be said to be complied with if the assessor can observe that the **procedure** contained in the organisation's documentation is in effective operation. All **procedures must** have a named person who is responsible for the **procedure**. They **must** also be reviewed at least annually.
Reasonable adjustments	The duty to make **reasonable adjustments** is a legal responsibility under anti-discrimination legislation. The requirement is intended to make sure that disabled people do not face difficulties in employment, education or when using services. A **reasonable adjustment** is a reasonable step taken to prevent a disabled person suffering a substantial disadvantage compared with people who are not disabled.
Register	Multiple records that are held in hard copy or electronic format.
Risk register	A **risk register** is a record of the risks facing the organisation or department. There is no fixed format for the **risk register** prescribed by Lexcel. It should indicate who has responsibility for a particular risk and any measures taken by the organisation or department to mitigate or reduce the risk.
Role profile	A description of the role undertaken by an individual including the key purpose of the role, summary of responsibilities and the skills and experience required of the individual.
Should	An optional requirement. In some cases, organisations or departments may be required to explain why they have chosen not to implement a requirement by their Lexcel assessor.
Strategic plan	A strategic plan is a plan that defines the organisation's goals and the activities required to achieve those goals.
Supervisor(s)	A person(s) who is (are) of sufficient seniority and in a position of sufficient responsibility with the appropriate skills and experience to guide and assist others.

1 STRUCTURE AND STRATEGY

1.1 The department *must* have documentation setting out the:

(a) management structure which designates the responsibilities of individuals and their accountability.

1.2 The department or its organisation *must* have a strategic *plan*. Where the department relies upon their organisation's strategic *plan* this *must* set out the departments' *objectives*. The *plan should* include:

(a) *objectives* for at least the next 12 months
(b) the identification of resources required to meet the *objectives*
(c) the services the department wishes to offer
(d) the client groups to be served
(e) how services will be delivered and marketed
(f) a documented risk *evaluation* of *objectives*
(g) *procedures* for regular reporting on performance.

1.3 The organisation *must* have a business continuity *plan* that encompasses the department, which *should* include:

(a) an *evaluation* of potential risks that could lead to business interruption
(b) ways to reduce, avoid and/or transfer the risks
(c) key people relevant to the implementation of the *plan*
(d) a *procedure* to test the *plan* annually, to verify that it would be effective in the event of a business interruption.

1.4 The department *should* have a *policy* in relation to *corporate social responsibility*.

2 FINANCIAL MANAGEMENT

2.1 The organisation *must* document the person who has overall responsibility for financial management of the department.

2.2 The department *should* be able to provide documentary evidence of their financial management *procedure*, including:

(a) annual budget including income and expenditure
(b) variance analysis conducted at least quarterly of income and expenditure against budgets.

2.3 The department *should* have a time recording *procedure*.

2.4 If appropriate, the department *should* have a *procedure* in relation to billing clients which, *should* include:

(a) the frequency and terms for billing clients
(b) credit limits for new and existing clients
(c) debt management.

2.5 Departments handling financial transactions, *should* have a *procedure*, which *should* include:

(a) the transfer of funds
(b) the management of funds received by the department
(c) *authorisations*.

3 INFORMATION MANAGEMENT

3.1 The department or the organisation *must* have an information management and security *policy*, which *should* include:

(a) a *register* of relevant information assets
(b) *procedures* for the protection and security of the information assets
(c) *procedures* for the retention and disposal of information
(d) the use of firewalls
(e) *procedures* for the secure configuration of network devices
(f) *procedures* to manage user accounts
(g) *procedures* to detect and remove *malicious software*
(h) a *register* of all software used
(i) training for *personnel* on information security
(j) a *plan* for the updating and monitoring of software.

3.2 The organisation *must* have an e-mail *policy* that encompasses the department, or the department *must* have its own *policy,* which *should* include:

(a) the scope of permitted and prohibited use
(b) *procedures* for monitoring *personnel* using e-mail
(c) *procedures* for the storage and destruction of e-mails.

3.3 If the department is featured on the organisation's website, the department *must* be encompassed by the organisation's website management *policy*, which *must* include:

(a) consideration of accessibility requirements for disabled clients.

And *should* include:

(b) a *procedure* for content approval, publishing and removal
(c) the scope of permitted and prohibited content
(d) *procedures* for the management of its security.

3.4 The organisation *must* have an internet access *policy* that encompasses the department, or the department *must* have a *policy* that is particular to their department, this *should* include:

(a) the scope of permitted and prohibited use
(b) *procedures* for monitoring *personnel* accessing the internet.

3.5 If the department participates in social media, the organisation *must* have a social media *policy* that encompasses the department, or the department *must* have its own *policy*, which *should* include:

(a) a *procedure* for participating in social media on behalf of the organisation
(b) the scope of permitted and prohibited content.

3.6 The organisation or department *must* have:

(a) a *register* of each *plan, policy* and *procedure* that is contained in the Lexcel Standard
(b) the named person responsible for each *policy, plan* and *procedure* that is contained in the Lexcel Standard
(c) a *procedure* for the review of each *policy, plan* and *procedure* that is contained in the Lexcel Standard.

4 PEOPLE MANAGEMENT

4.1 The department or the organisation *must* have a health and safety *policy*.
4.2 The department or the organisation *must* have an equality and diversity *policy*, which *should* include:

(a) recruitment, selection and progression
(b) a *procedure* to deal with complaints and disciplinary issues in breach of the *policy*
(c) a *procedure* to monitor diversity and collate equality data
(d) training of all *personnel* on compliance with equality and diversity requirements
(e) *procedures* for *reasonable adjustments* for *personnel*.

4.3 The department *must* be encompassed by the organisation's learning and development *policy*, which *should* include:

(a) ensuring that appropriate training is provided to *personnel*
(b) ensuring that all *supervisors* and managers receive appropriate training
(c) a *procedure* to evaluate training
(d) a learning and development *plan* for all *personnel*.

4.4 The organisation or department *must* list the tasks to be undertaken by all *personnel* within the department usually in the form of a *role profile*.
4.5 The department *must* be encompassed by the organisation's *procedures* to deal effectively with recruitment selection and progression, or have *procedures* particular to the department, which *should* include:

(a) the identification of vacancies
(b) the drafting of the job documentation
(c) methods of attracting candidates
(d) clear and transparent selection
(e) storage, retention and destruction of records
(f) references and ID checking
(g) where appropriate, the checking of disciplinary records.

4.6 The department *must* be encompassed by the organisation's induction arrangements for *personnel*, or have arrangements particular to the department, including those transferring roles within the organisation and *should* cover:

(a) the management structure and the individual's responsibilities
(b) terms and conditions of employment
(c) immediate training requirements
(d) key *policies*.

4.7 **The department or the organisation *must* have a *procedure* which details the steps to be followed when a member of *personnel* ceases to be an employee, which *should* include:**

(a) the handover of work
(b) exit interviews
(c) the return of property belonging to the organisation.

4.8 **The department *must* be encompassed by the organisation's performance management *policy* or have a *policy* that is particular to the department, which *should* include:**

(a) the organisation or department's approach to performance management
(b) performance review periods and timescales.

4.9 **The department or the organisation *must* have a whistleblowing *policy*.**
4.10 **The department or the organisation *must* have a *flexible working policy*.**

5 RISK MANAGEMENT

5.1 **The department *must* be encompassed by the organisation's risk management *policy*, or have a *policy* that is particular to the department, which *should* include:**

(a) a compliance *plan*, if relevant
(b) a *risk register*
(c) defined risk management roles and responsibilities
(d) arrangements for communicating risk information.

5.2 **The department *must* be encompassed by the organisation's outsourced activities *policy* or have a *policy* that is particular to the department, which *should* include:**

(a) details of all outsourced activities including providers
(b) *procedures* to check the quality of outsourced work
(c) *procedures* to ensure providers have taken appropriate precautions to ensure information will be protected.

5.3 **There *must* be a named *supervisor* for each area of work undertaken by the department.**
5.4 **The department *must* have *procedures* to manage instructions which may be undertaken even though they have a higher *risk profile*, including unusual supervisory and reporting requirements or contingency planning.**
5.5 **The department *should* maintain lists of work that it will and will not undertake. This information *should* be communicated to all relevant *personnel* and *should* be updated when changes occur.**
5.6 **If the department acts for or advises *external clients*, they *must* maintain details of the generic risks and causes of claims associated with the area(s) of work undertaken by the department. This information *must* be communicated to all relevant *personnel*.**
5.7 **The department *must* have a *procedure* to monitor key dates, or be encompassed by the organisation's *procedure*, which *must* include:**

(a) the definition of key dates by work type for the department
(b) ensuring that key dates are recorded on the file and in a back-up system.

5.8 **The department *must* be encompassed by the organisation's *policy* on the handling of conflicts, or have a *policy* that is particular to the department, which *should* include:**

(a) the definition of conflicts
(b) training for all relevant *personnel* to identify conflicts
(c) steps to be followed when a conflict is identified.

5.9 The department *must* be encompassed by the organisation's *procedure* to ensure that all *personnel*, both permanent and temporary, are actively supervised, or have *procedures* that are particular to their department. Such *procedures must* include:

(a) checks on incoming and outgoing correspondence, where appropriate
(b) departmental, team and office meetings and communication structures, where appropriate
(c) reviews of matter details in order to ensure good financial controls and the appropriate allocation of workloads, where appropriate
(d) the exercise of devolved powers in publicly funded work, where appropriate
(e) the availability of a *supervisor*
(f) allocation of new work and reallocation of existing work, if necessary.

5.10 The department *must* have a *procedure* to ensure that all those doing legal work check their files regularly for inactivity.

5.11 The department *must* have a *procedure* for regular, independent file reviews of either the management of the file or its substantive legal content, or both. In relation to file reviews, the department *must*:

(a) define and explain file selection criteria
(b) define and explain the number and frequency of reviews
(c) retain a record of the file review on the matter file and centrally
(d) ensure any corrective action, which is identified in a file review, is acted upon within 28 days and verified
(e) ensure that the designated *supervisor* reviews and monitors the data generated by file reviews
(f) conduct a review at least annually of the data generated by file reviews.

5.12 Operational risk *must* be considered and recorded in all matters before, during and after the processing of instructions. Before the matter is undertaken the legal advisor *must*:

(a) consider if a new client and/or matter is accepted by the department, in accordance with section 6.1 and 6.7 below
(b) assess the risk profile of all new instructions and notify the *supervisor,* in accordance with *procedures* under 5.4, of any unusual or high risk considerations in order that appropriate action may be taken.

During the retainer the legal advisor *must*:

(c) consider any change to the *risk profile* of the matter and report and advise on such circumstances without delay, informing the *supervisor* if appropriate
(d) inform the client in all cases where an adverse costs order is made against the organisation in relation to the matter in question.

At the end of the matter the legal advisor *must*:

(e) undertake a concluding risk assessment by considering if the client's *objectives* have been achieved
(f) notify the *supervisor* of all such circumstances in accordance with documented *procedures* in section 5.4 above.

5.13 **If anti-money laundering legislation applies to the organisation, the department *must* be encompassed by the organisation's anti-money laundering *policy* or have a *policy* that is particular to the department, which *must* include:**

(a) the appointment of a nominated officer usually referred to as a Money Laundering Reporting Officer (MLRO)
(b) a *procedure* for making disclosures within the organisation and by the MLRO to the authorities
(c) a *procedure* for checking the identity of the department's clients, if appropriate
(d) a *plan* for the training of *personnel*
(e) *procedures* for the proper maintenance of records.

5.14 **The department *must* be encompassed by the organisation's *policy* setting out the *procedures* to prevent bribery in accordance with current legislation or have a *policy* particular to the department.**

5.15 **The department *must* be included in the organisation's analysis of risk assessment data that is generated or undertake an analysis of risk data particular to their department. This *should* include:**

(a) any indemnity insurance claims (where applicable)
(b) an analysis of client complaints trends
(c) data generated by file reviews
(d) any breaches that have been notified to the SRA
(e) situations where the department acted where a conflict existed (where applicable)
(f) the identification of remedial action.

6 CLIENT CARE

6.1 **The department *must* have a *policy* for client care, which *should* include:**

(a) how enquiries from potential clients will be dealt with
(b) ensuring that before taking on a client, the department has sufficient resources and competence to deal with the matter
(c) protecting client confidentiality
(d) a timely response is made to telephone calls and correspondence from the client and others
(e) a *procedure* for referring clients to third parties
(f) the provision of *reasonable adjustments* for disabled clients.

6.2 **The department *must* communicate the following to clients in writing, unless an alternative form of communication is deemed more appropriate:**

(a) where appropriate, establish the client's requirements and *objectives*
(b) provide a clear explanation of the issues involved and the options available to the client
(c) explain what the legal advisor will and will not do
(d) agree with the client the next steps to be taken
(e) keep the client informed of progress, as agreed
(f) establish in what timescale that matter will be dealt with
(g) where appropriate, establish the method of funding
(h) where appropriate, consider whether the intended action would be merited on a cost benefit analysis
(i) agree an appropriate level of service

(j) explain the department's responsibilities and the client's
(k) provide the client with the name and status of the person dealing with their matter
(l) where appropriate, the client is given the name and status of the person responsible for the overall supervision of their matter.

6.3 Where appropriate, the department *should* have a service level or similar agreements with their client departments.

6.4 Where appropriate, the department *must* give clients the best information possible about the likely overall cost of the matter, both at the outset and when appropriate, as the matter progresses, in particular the department *should*:

(a) advise the client of the basis of the department's charging
(b) advise the client where the organisation will receive a financial benefit as a result of accepting instructions
(c) advise the client if the charging rates are to be increased
(d) advise the client of likely payments which the department or the client may need to make to others
(e) discuss with the client how they will pay
(f) advise the client that there are circumstances where the department may be entitled to exercise a lien for unpaid costs
(g) advise the client of their potential liability for any other party's costs.

6.5 The department *must* be encompassed by the organisation's complaints handling *procedure* or have a *procedure* particular to the department, which *should* include:

(a) the definition of what the organisation regards as a complaint
(b) informing the client at the outset of the matter, that in the event of a problem they are entitled to complain
(c) the name of the person with overall responsibility for complaints
(d) providing the client with a copy of the organisation's or department's complaints *procedure*, if requested
(e) once a complaint has been made, the person complaining is informed in writing:

(i) how the complaint will be handled; and
(ii) in what time they will be given an initial and/or substantive response

(f) recording and reporting centrally all complaints received from clients
(g) identifying the cause of any problems of which the client has complained, offering any appropriate redress, and correcting any unsatisfactory *procedures*.

6.6 The department *must* be encompassed by the organisation's *procedure* to monitor client satisfaction or have a *procedure* that is particular to the department.

6.7 Where appropriate, the department *must* have a *procedure* to accept or decline instructions, which *should* include:

(a) how decisions are made to accept instructions from new and existing clients
(b) how decisions are made to stop acting for an existing client
(c) how decisions are made to decline instructions.

7 FILE AND CASE MANAGEMENT

7.1 The department *must* ensure that the strategy for a matter is always apparent on the matter file and that in complex cases a project plan is developed.

7.2 The department *must* document *procedures* for the giving, monitoring and discharge of undertakings.

7.3 The department *must* be encompassed by the organisation's *procedure* or have a *procedure* particular to the department to:

(a) list open and closed matters
(b) ensure that they are able to identify and trace any documents, files, deeds, wills or any other items relating to the matter
(c) safeguard the confidentiality of matter files and all other client information
(d) ensure that the status of the matter and the action taken can be easily checked by other members of the department
(e) ensure that documents are stored on the matter file(s) in an orderly way.

7.4 The department will have *procedures* to ensure that matters are progressed in an appropriate manner. In particular:

(a) key information *must* be recorded on the file
(b) a timely response is made to telephone calls and correspondence from the client and others
(c) where appropriate, continuing cost information is provided
(d) clients are informed in writing if the person with conduct of their matter changes, or there is a change of person to whom any problem with service may be addressed.

7.5 The department *must* be encompassed by the organisation's documented *procedure* for using barristers, expert witnesses and other external advisers who are involved in the delivery of legal services, or have a *procedure* particular to the department, which *should* include provision for the following:

(a) use of clear selection criteria in line with the equality and diversity *policy*
(b) where appropriate, consult with the client in relation to selection of advocate or other professional
(c) advising the clients of the name and status of the person being instructed, how long she/he might take to respond and, where disbursements are to be paid by the client, the cost involved
(d) maintenance of records on barristers and experts used, including evidence of assessment against the criteria
(e) *evaluation* of performance, for the information of other members of the department or organisation
(f) giving clear instructions
(g) checking of opinions and reports received to ensure they adequately provide the information sought (and, in litigation matters, comply with the rules of court and any court orders)
(h) payment of fees.

7.6 The department *must* have *procedures* to ensure that, at the end of the matter, the department:

(a) if required, reports to the client on the outcome and explains any further action that the client is required to take in the matter and what (if anything) the department will do
(b) where appropriate, accounts to the client for any outstanding money
(c) returns to the client any original documents or other property belonging to the client, if required

(d) if appropriate, advises the client about arrangements for storage and retrieval of papers and other items retained (in so far as this has not already been dealt with, for example, in terms of business) and any charges to be made in this regard

(e) advises the client whether it is appropriate to review the matter in future and, if so, when and why

(f) archives and destroys files in an appropriate manner.

Assessment criteria

1 STRUCTURE AND STRATEGY

1.1 The department *must* have documentation setting out the:

(a) management structure which designates the responsibilities of individuals and their accountability.

The management structure may apply just to a department or to the whole of the organisation of which it forms part. This information may be presented in a wide variety of forms, for example, in an organisational chart and/or in personnel profiles on the intranet.

> **Assessment note:** Departments should be able to produce documentary evidence of the management structure which designates the responsibilities of individuals and their accountability. In addition to having access to the documentation, assessors will gather interview evidence to confirm that the management structure and the responsibilities within departments are understood by personnel.

1.2 The department or its organisation *must* have a strategic *plan*. Where the department relies upon their organisation's strategic *plan* this *must* set out the departments' *objectives*. The *plan should* include:

(a) *objectives* for at least the next 12 months
(b) the identification of resources required to meet the *objectives*
(c) the services the department wishes to offer
(d) the client groups to be served
(e) how services will be delivered and marketed
(f) a documented risk *evaluation* of *objectives*
(g) *procedures* for regular reporting on performance.

If departments have a departmental plan or contribute significantly to their organisation's strategic plan, then they should be aware that strategy is dynamic in nature and that a strategic plan should be regularly reviewed and updated.

Departments are required to review their plan at least annually. However, the frequency of review should take into consideration macro environmental factors and internal changes within departments or their organisation, which may impact on their organisation's ability to meet its set objectives. Therefore, departments should avoid using the review period simply to meet Lexcel requirements and instead ensure that the review period takes into consideration changes that may impact on a department's ability to meet its objectives.

When setting objectives, departments should consider using the SMART (Specific, Measureable, Achievable, Realistic, Time-bound) format. An example of a SMART objective would be to reduce to two days the time between a client making contact with a department and being allocated a legal advisor, which is to be introduced/implemented within the next six months.

As part of the process of setting the strategy, departments should consider their current resources and then identify any gaps that they need to address in order to meet their objectives. The main resources to consider are:

- people (HR);
- finance;
- technology; and
- facilities.

Departments should consider using a SWOT (Strengths, Weaknesses, Opportunities and Threats) analysis to assist them in understanding their department and evaluating risk, as required by 1.2(f).

There are other forms of analysis that departments can undertake such as PEST (Political, Environment, Social and Technological), which may be helpful when developing their department's strategy and understanding risks.

Internal clients: Departments must have a documented strategic plan or be included in their organisation's strategic plan, ensuring that their objectives are defined for at least the next 12 months.

The requirements in 1.2(a)–(g) are not necessarily appropriate as many departments only advise and act for internal clients and so may have little choice over the services they wish to offer and the client groups to be served. Therefore, not all of the requirements in 1.2 may be directly relevant to every department. In the scenario described above it is acceptable for the departments to disregard the requirements set out in 1.2(a)–(g). Departments do not need to document the reasons why they believe that the requirements are not appropriate but departments should be able to explain their decision to their assessor.

External clients: The objectives referred to at 1.2(a) should include information concerning marketing activities if departments propose to deliver legal advice to new clients.

As part of a department's strategy and business planning, particularly in defining target groups and geographical locations, departments may outline plans to promote access to their services by diverse groups, taking account of language, cultural background, religion and disability.

If equality, diversity and inclusion initiatives are part of a department's strategy to win new business or to develop its existing client base, the strategy and business plan should identify ways in which the department can participate in such initiatives in the local and wider community. Ideally, the department should indicate the steps that have been taken towards reaching this goal. This could also be included as part of an organisation's corporate social responsibility (CSR) policy (see 1.4).

Departments that act for external clients should refer to the guidance notes at 1.2 of the standard for legal practices, as it is likely that departments will benefit from meeting the requirements as set out for legal practices.

Assessment note: It is acknowledged that not all of the requirements in 1.2 will be directly relevant to all departments. It is acceptable for departments to disregard the requirements set out in 1.2(a)–(g). Although departments are not required to document the reasons for their choice, they must be able to explain to their assessor the reason why they consider the subclauses to be irrelevant.

Assessors are likely to require a greater level of interview evidence for those departments that advise and act for external clients.

1.3 The organisation *must* have a business continuity *plan* that encompasses the department, which *should* include:

(a) an *evaluation* of potential risks that could lead to business interruption
(b) ways to reduce, avoid and/or transfer the risks
(c) key people relevant to the implementation of the *plan*
(d) a *procedure* to test the *plan* annually, to verify that it would be effective in the event of a business interruption.

If departments have a separate business continuity plan (BCP) or significantly contribute to their organisation's BCP, the key areas of risk that should be addressed in the plan are as follows:

- Geographic location (flood, fire, terrorist attacks).
- Loss of key personnel.
- Loss of facilities (IT, access to the building).

Departments should identify what the risks are, for example, the organisation's/department's physical location and the specific risks associated with that location. Departments should then evaluate the potential risks that have been identified that could lead to business interruptions as required by 1.3(a).

The next step is to assess the likelihood of a risk occurring and its impact. Following this process should help departments to prioritise the risks and decide upon how to mitigate them. When addressing requirement 1.3(b), departments may wish to tabulate this information.

Testing the BCP is one of the most valuable and challenging aspects thereof. The purpose of testing the BCP is to identify possible weaknesses and rectify these before a real incident occurs. Departments must document both the BCP and how it is tested.

There are a range of methods that departments can use to test the BCP. One of the most frequently used methods is desktop testing. This involves creating a scenario and asking participants to discuss the steps to be taken in accordance with the BCP.

In addition to the scheduled testing of the BCP, departments may draw upon their experience of actual interruptions to their organisation's business within the last 12 months and the lessons learned from such interruptions and whether any changes were made to the BCP as a result.

Best practice is to keep copies of the BCP away from the office, such as at the homes of members of personnel and to include key information to facilitate departments and their organisations getting back to business as usual, as soon as possible, including, for example, building insurance contact details.

The Law Society produces a free practice note in relation to business continuity, which can be accessed at **www.lawsociety.org.uk/advice/practice-notes/business-continuity**.

Internal clients: Departments may be encompassed by their organisation's BCP or have their own plan.

Some departments may not directly feature in their organisation's plan with little or no direct reference being made to them therein.

External clients: If departments act for external clients it is recommended that they comply with the requirements in 1.3(a)–(d), as far as possible. However, it is recognised that departments may have organisational constraints that prevent them from fully meeting all of these requirements.

1.4 The department *should* have a *policy* in relation to *corporate social responsibility*.

Departments may be encompassed by their organisation's CSR policy or have their own policy.

This requirement is optional. If a department is part of a charitable organisation, a CSR policy may be at the very heart of the organisation and should be documented.

Typically, the issues that departments may want to incorporate into the policy include:

- facilities;
- recycling;
- resources;
- travel; and
- pro bono and charitable work.

Assessment note: As this is an optional requirement, assessors will not raise non-compliances against this requirement.

2 FINANCIAL MANAGEMENT

2.1 The organisation *must* document the person who has overall responsibility for financial management of the department.

Departments may wish to document the person responsible for the financial management of their department as part of the requirement at 1.1.

The person who is responsible for the financial management of a department does not have to be a member of that department. However, they may be part of another department within the organisation. Departments must be able to identify who has overall responsibility for the financial management of their department. It is acceptable to name either the person or the role for the purposes of Lexcel. For example, a department may state that the head of its department is the person responsible for the financial management thereof. There may be some organisations where a committee is responsible for the financial management of a department. It is acceptable for the committee or chairperson of the committee to be identified.

> **Assessment note:** A department may refer to the person with responsibility for overall financial management in an organisational chart, or a departmental or organisational manual. Alternatively, the information may be found on the intranet or within a job description.

2.2 The department *should* be able to provide documentary evidence of their financial management *procedure*, including:

(a) annual budget including income and expenditure
(b) variance analysis conducted at least quarterly of income and expenditure against budgets.

Responsibility for a department's financial management may reside outside the department.

Budgets are a means of communicating to managers the resources available to deliver their services. Budgets are most commonly expressed in financial terms. However, departments may wish to include non-financial terms, such as the number of clients they wish to deliver their services to. Budgets are also a crucial part of a department's planning and control mechanism. Ideally, budgets should forecast not simply what is expected, but also what the department wants to achieve.

The majority of departments will usually have an allocated budget or may be in the process of bidding for a budget or funding and must produce this information to their assessor. However, there may be some departments that do not have an allocated budget or the legal advisors may be part of a wider department. In these circumstances, departments will not need to comply with these requirements.

The variance analysis that is referred to in 2.2(b) relates to the difference between the budgeted/forecast figures and the actual figures. Conducting the variance analysis will help departments to understand whether or not they are meeting their financial budgets and targets.

Assessment note: Assessors will need to be satisfied that a department has procedures in place to manage its financial information. Departments may provide an assessor with copies of the budget and variance analysis or interview evidence.

2.3 The department *should* have a time recording *procedure*.

This is an optional requirement. However, time recording can provide valuable management information, particularly in relation to the productivity and performance of personnel. Therefore consideration should be given as to whether or not time recording by legal advisors may be beneficial.

External clients: This is an optional requirement. However, if departments bill clients on a time basis it is crucial to accurately record time.

Assessment note: As this is an optional requirement, assessors should not raise non-compliances against this requirement.

2.4 If appropriate, the department *should* have a *procedure* in relation to billing clients which *should* include:

(a) the frequency and terms for billing clients
(b) credit limits for new and existing clients
(c) debt management.

Internal clients: If departments act for internal clients and do not have billing arrangements in place, they can disregard these requirements as they are not applicable to such departments.

External clients: If departments advise or act for external clients and bill these clients, they should ensure that client expectations are managed from the outset in relation to 2.4(a).

Credit limits in 2.4(b) usually refer to the value of work that departments are willing to undertake before issuing their client with a bill. It is acceptable to set out a general procedure for all clients or matter types or decide this on a case-by-case basis.

2.4(c) requires departments to set out the steps to be taken in the event that a bill is not paid on time.

It is accepted that acting for external clients does not automatically necessitate billing clients, for example, many not-for-profit organisations that offer legal services do not bill their clients. In these circumstances departments would not need to comply with 2.4.

Assessment note: Assessors will take into consideration a department's specific circumstances and the client groups that it serves. Departments will need to be able to demonstrate by interview evidence that the issues in 2.4 have been considered.

2.5 Departments handling financial transactions, *should* have a *procedure*, which should include:

(a) the transfer of funds
(b) the management of funds received by the department
(c) *authorisations*.

Departments are only required to have a procedure if they handle financial transactions. For example, legal advisors may be required to authorise payments. However, if a department does not handle financial transactions then it may disregard the requirements under 2.5.

Assessment note: Departments will need to explain, at the assessment, why the requirements in 2.5 do not apply to them. However, it is not necessary for departments to document this decision.

3 INFORMATION MANAGEMENT

3.1 The department or the organisation *must* have an information management and security *policy*, which *should* include:

(a) a *register* of relevant information assets
(b) *procedures* for the protection and security of the information assets
(c) *procedures* for the retention and disposal of information
(d) the use of firewalls
(e) *procedures* for the secure configuration of network devices
(f) *procedures* to manage user accounts
(g) *procedures* to detect and remove *malicious software*
(h) a *register* of all software used
(i) training for *personnel* on information security
(j) a *plan* for the updating and monitoring of software.

The information management and security policy essentially needs to address how the department and/or organisation ensures that information is kept confidential, its integrity is maintained and it is accessible. This is critical on a day-to-day basis and also needs to be considered in the context of the business continuity requirements that are set out in 1.3. The policy must encompass information that is held electronically and physically. The requirements of 3.1(a)–(j) provide a framework to address the key issues that will help the department/organisation form its policy. Although the subclauses of 3.1 are optional, to reflect that some departments will be bound by an organisation-wide policy that does not necessarily adopt the same subclauses as Lexcel, it is unlikely that the department or organisation will have an effective policy unless it addresses all of the subclauses in 3.1.

To create the information asset register as required by 3.1(a), the department/organisation needs to define what an information asset is. One method the department/organisation may wish to consider adopting is to analyse the value of the information by assessing the impact its loss would have. This should help to decide whether the information is an asset and needs to be included in the register.

The most effective means of protecting information assets evolves as risks change, particularly in relation to information that is held electronically. The department/organisation is encouraged to regularly review the procedures it adopts to meet 3.1(b) as threats change. The government has introduced the Cyber Essentials Scheme to help businesses deal with cyber security issues. To find out more information about the scheme, please visit **www.gov.uk/government/publications/cyber-essentials-scheme-overview**.

The Law Society also provides an online training course which deals with cyber security issues. This free online training can be accessed at **http://cpdcentre.lawsociety.org.uk/course/6707/cyber-security-for-legal-and-accountancy-professionals**.

In addition, there is an international standard for information security, ISO 27001, to which departments/organisations may wish to consider aligning or gaining accreditation. More information is available at **www.iso.org/iso/home/standards/management-standards/iso27001.htm**.

When formulating the policy in relation to 3.1(c), the department/organisation should ensure that it is consistent with 4.5(e) and 7.6(f).

One of the key weaknesses in any department's/organisation's armour in respect of threats is personnel not understanding the policy and allowing threats to bypass the safeguards that have been put in place. Training personnel to a high standard should ensure that they understand the policy and provide a robust defence to potential threats. For example departments/organisations may have very effective firewalls, but, if social engineering techniques enable a criminal to persuade a member of personnel to insert a memory stick into his or her computer and unwittingly introduce malware, the investment in technology would have been somewhat wasted.

The data protection legislation is also a theme that the department/organisation needs to encompass within the policy. The department/organisation may wish to access the Law Society practice note on data protection, which is available at **www.lawsociety.org.uk/advice/practice-notes/data-protection**.

There are also Law Society practice notes on information security and cloud computing that departments may wish to consider. These can be accessed at the following:

- **www.lawsociety.org.uk/advice/practice-notes/information-security**.
- **www.lawsociety.org.uk/advice/practice-notes/cloud-computing**.

Assessment note: Assessors will need to have access to the documented policy. It is not mandatory for all the subclauses to be met. However, where they are not complied with, assessors will seek to understand why they are not appropriate and the steps taken to influence the wider organisation, where possible, to adhere to good practice.

3.2 The organisation *must* have an e-mail *policy* that encompasses the department, or the department *must* have its own *policy*, which *should* include:

(a) the scope of permitted and prohibited use
(b) *procedures* for monitoring *personnel* using e-mail
(c) *procedures* for the storage and destruction of e-mails.

It is likely that departments will be bound by an organisational e-mail policy. However, if an organisational policy does not exist then the department must have its own policy.

It is also possible that the e-mail policy may form part of the information management and security policy or be a standalone policy. How the department decides to deal with the requirements in 3.2 is a matter of preference and it will be compliant, as the department may be bound by an organisation-wide policy. It is not mandatory to comply with the subclauses in 3.2.

3.2(b) does not require a department/organisation to monitor e-mails, only that it sets out what its policy is in relation to monitoring. Therefore, a department/organisation may or may not choose to monitor e-mails. This information should be communicated to personnel via the policy.

In the event that a department/organisation does monitor personnel e-mails, it should be mindful of privacy issues and ensure that it takes a proportionate approach and takes steps to ensure that personnel are aware that it monitors e-mails. Care must be taken to comply with current regulations. Departments/organisations may wish to consult the Information Commissioner's guidance on monitoring employee e-mails to ensure that their policy is in compliance with relevant legislation.

It is considered good practice to set out the consequences of personnel breaching the e-mail policy. For example, whether a breach of the e-mail policy would lead to disciplinary action.

When it drafts the policy in relation to 3.2(c), a department/organisation should consider whether it is consistent with 3.1(c), 4.5(e) and 7.6(f).

3.3 If the department is featured on the organisation's website, the department *must* be encompassed by the organisation's website management *policy*, which *must* include:

(a) consideration of accessibility requirements for disabled clients.

And *should* include:

(b) a *procedure* for content approval, publishing and removal
(c) the scope of permitted and prohibited content
(d) *procedures* for the management of its security.

If the department is featured on the organisation's website and is required to contribute to the website management policy, the following may be of assistance.

For the majority of departments they will have little input into the website management policy. However in the event that a department is required to assist with the drafting of the website policy, the department needs to consider what the purpose of the website is.

3.3(b) is primarily focused on the systems level and requires a department/organisation to consider issues concerning how content for the website will be approved, published and removed. Roles and responsibilities as well as the budget should be considered at this stage. The procedures should include a check to ensure that the website is fulfilling the needs of the end user, particularly in relation to disabled clients, as required by 3.3(a); for example, whether there are any measures in place to test the website's usability for visually impaired clients. It is also critical to ensure that the website is compliant from a legal and regulatory perspective. Therefore the policy should include the following issues:

- Copyright.
- Data protection.
- Defamation.
- Electronic commerce.
- Distance selling.
- Equality and diversity.

The organisation will need to provide guidance to personnel that are involved in the creation and updating of the website. 3.3(c) requires organisations to provide guidance to personnel that are involved in the creation and updating of the website.

The requirement at 3.3(d) must be consistent with the information management and security policy. This may form part of such policy or be part of a general communications policy. Lexcel does not set out a particular format that should be used, only that the requirement must be complied with. A department/organisation will need to set out the steps it has in place to safeguard the confidentiality of the website data.

The integrity of a department's/organisation's website is another strand to the security of its website that needs to be incorporated into the policy. Technical safeguards need to be in place to prevent attackers being able to make changes to the website, as well as effectively managing issues such as disabling former employees' access, so that they can no longer make changes to the website.

One of the most frequent types of attack on websites revolves around them being taken offline. Departments/organisations may wish to access the Department for Business, Innovation and Skills' *10 Steps to Cyber Security* for additional guidance on information security and websites.

Assessment note: If a department is not featured on the website and has no input into the website management policy, its assessor will accept that it is not applicable to the department. However, if the department does feature on the website, its assessor will look to the organisation's website management policy to understand the role of the department.

Internal clients: It is unlikely that a department that advises and acts for internal clients will be featured on the organisation's website. Therefore 3.3 is unlikely to be relevant to the department in such circumstances.

External clients: This requirement does not make it mandatory to have a website. However, if the department or organisation does have a website then the department/organisation must ensure that it is managed in accordance with the policy. 3.3(d) relates to information security and therefore the department/organisation should ensure that the policy in 3.3 is consistent with 3.1.

In order to meet the requirements of 3.3(a) the department/organisation may wish to access the following information:

- How to meet Web Content Accessibility Guidelines 2.0: **www.w3.org/WAI/WCAG20/quickref**.
- A guide to understanding and implementing Web Content Accessibility Guidelines 2.0: **www.w3.org/TR/UNDERSTANDING-WCAG20**.

3.4 The organisation *must* have an internet access *policy* that encompasses the department, or the department *must* have a *policy* that is particular to their department, this *should* include:

(a) the scope of permitted and prohibited use
(b) *procedures* for monitoring *personnel* accessing the internet.

It is likely that departments will be subject to their organisation's policy. However if there is not an organisation-wide policy the department must have its own policy. This policy may form part of the information security and information management policy, or an electronic communications policy, or a standalone policy. Issues such as downloading information and programs should be addressed in the policy.

3.4(b) does not require departments/organisations to monitor personnel accessing the internet. However, the policy must state whether or not the organisation monitors internet use. If a organisation chooses to monitor internet use, then it must ensure that it considers an individual's right to privacy and it must take a proportional approach. There is the possibility of using software to assist with monitoring. Departments/organisations may wish to access further guidance in relation to monitoring personnel by visiting the Information Commissioner's Office website, to help ensure that the policy complies with current legislation and good practice (**http://ico.org.uk**).

Assessment note: Assessors will need to review the policy, whether it is an organisation-wide policy or departmental policy. Assessors will then seek interview evidence to verify that it is understood and in effective operation.

3.5 If the department participates in social media, the organisation *must* have a social media *policy* that encompasses the department, or the department *must* have its own *policy*, which *should* include:

(a) a *procedure* for participating in social media on behalf of the organisation
(b) the scope of permitted and prohibited content.

It is likely that the department will be encompassed by the organisation's policy. Some organisations host workshops for personnel to help design the policy. As with all policies, a good starting point is to consider what the department/organisation wants the policy to achieve. The social media policy should also be consistent with the policy at 3.1. Social media is a dynamic form of communication and the policy will need to reflect the level of access for members of personnel. For example, whether a department/organisation encourages all personnel to participate in social media to raise its profile or whether there are designated personnel that are permitted to participate on its behalf. Clear guidelines need to be set out and understood by members of personnel. It is likely that a department/organisation would want social media to enhance its reputation and avoid potential damage to the same. Therefore the policy should address key issues, such as:

- scope of the policy;
- roles and responsibilities;
- forms of social media;
- how the policy applies to business and personal use;
- consequences of breaching the policy; and
- how to give feedback on the policy.

As with other policies, it is considered good practice to incorporate the social media policy into conditions of employment and include it as part of the induction. This helps to ensure that all personnel are aware of and understand the policy. In addition, departments/organisations may want to set out the potential penalties for misuse.

Internal clients: It is unlikely that a department that advises and acts for internal clients will participate in social media, therefore 3.5 is unlikely to be relevant to such departments.

Assessment note: Assessors will review the documented policy and ensure that it is understood by the personnel that are interviewed.

3.6 The *organisation* or department *must* have:

- **(a) a *register* of each *plan, policy* and *procedure* that is contained in the Lexcel Standard**
- **(b) the named person responsible for each *policy, plan* and *procedure* that is contained in the Lexcel Standard**
- **(c) a *procedure* for the review of each *policy, plan* and *procedure* that is contained in the Lexcel Standard.**

The requirements of 3.6 apply to all plans, policies and procedures in sections 1 to 7 of the Standard. Generally, the register will include the following information:

- The name of the person responsible.
- The name of the document.
- The date that the document was created.
- The date that the document was last updated.
- The frequency of review.

Issues that a department/organisation may wish to include in the review procedure are as follows:

- Whether there have been any breaches.
- Whether there have been any near breaches.
- Whether the law or regulations have changed in this area.
- Whether lines of accountability or reporting have changed.
- Whether a department/organisation is satisfied that the plan, policy or procedure is fit for purpose.

> **Assessment note:** Assessors will review the register and ensure that the annual reviews have taken place. The department/organisation may document the substance of the annual review, in an alternative form, for example, in the minutes of meetings.

4 PEOPLE MANAGEMENT

4.1 The department or the organisation *must* have a health and safety *policy*.

There are legal duties on employers and organisations to ensure a safe working environment. In accordance with the applicable legislation, a department should be encompassed by the organisation's health and safety policy. In the absence of an organisation-wide policy, a department will be required to have its own documented policy. A good source of information is the Health and Safety Executive's website at **www.hse.gov.uk**.

In the event that a department is required to draft a health and safety policy, it should take steps to ensure that the policy sets out its commitment to managing health and safety effectively, and what it intends to achieve. It should be apparent from the policy who is responsible for the policy and the specific actions required to meet its obligations.

In addition, departments should provide details of what they intend to do on a day-to-day basis to achieve the aims set out in their health and safety policy.

Departments should consider the following issues when forming their policy:

- Equipment that may be used by personnel.
- Personnel handling and using substances.
- Accidents, first aid and work-related ill health.
- Monitoring of conditions and systems of work.
- Emergency procedures, fire and evacuation of premises.
- Home working.
- Lone working.
- Meeting clients away from the office.
- Stress management.
- Visitors to the premises, including clients and third parties.

> **Assessment note:** Assessors will seek evidence that the policy is working effectively by verifying that the policy is documented and confirming through interview evidence that personnel understand the policy. Assessors should not require departments to include all of the issues set out above as they may not be appropriate for some departments.

4.2 The department or the organisation *must* have an equality and diversity *policy*, which *should* include:

(a) recruitment, selection and progression
(b) a *procedure* to deal with complaints and disciplinary issues in breach of the *policy*
(c) a *procedure* to monitor diversity and collate equality data
(d) training of all *personnel* on compliance with equality and diversity requirements
(e) *procedures* for *reasonable adjustments* for *personnel*.

A department's or organisation's equality and diversity policy must cover recruitment, selection, progression, retention and pay. A department or its organisation should have regard to outcomes 2.1 and 2.2 of the SRA Code of Conduct 2011, principle 9 of the SRA Principles and equality legislation to ensure that its policy is effective.

The policy should cover both existing and new personnel and should be made available to all personnel in the department. This can be achieved by publishing it on the organisation's website or by making it a part of the departmental manual or an induction/introductory pack provided to all personnel.

A department/organisation should monitor its equality and diversity policy on a regular basis to ensure it is being complied with. This review must take place at least annually.

An annual survey, whether online or document-based, can help a department to collect diversity data. The SRA has issued a model questionnaire to be used for the collection of diversity data, which can be found on the SRA's website.

Individual personnel are under no obligation to disclose their data. They can state that they would prefer not to say and should not be forced or pressurised into providing data. However, it is considered to be good practice to encourage personnel to complete the survey.

Departments should publish the diversity data that they have collected, but only where in doing so they do not breach confidentiality. This means that where there is a small group of personnel (e.g. fewer than 10) in any given diversity category, a department should only publish if it has the explicit consent of everyone who has provided the data. Departments may choose the form in which they publish the data, for example on an organisation's website, as a printed handout or on a notice in the reception area. The key issue is ensuring that it is readily available.

The collected diversity data should be used by a department/organisation to analyse the composition of its workforce by diversity, in comparison to relevant baseline data (for example, data from the Law Society on the diversity profile of the profession and official diversity statistics on the working age profile in the area/region in which an organisation is based) and to identify any under-representation. The department/organisation should also use the data to review its recruitment, selection and promotion procedures to ensure that these are fair and that under-represented groups are encouraged to apply.

Diversity training must be provided to all personnel. Such training must set out the equality and diversity requirements and inform personnel about their individual and collective duties.

A department/organisation must be aware of its obligations to ensure reasonable adjustments are made for disabled employees in accordance with outcome 2.3 of the SRA Code of Conduct 2011 and principle 9 of the SRA Principles. The equality and diversity policy should set out what steps a department/organisation intends to take to identify and manage reasonable adjustment requests from personnel who have a disability. A list of the types of adjustment a department/organisation can offer may be included in the policy.

Assessment note: Assessors will seek documentary and interview evidence that the policy is working effectively by verifying that the policy addresses key issues and is understood by personnel.

4.3 The department *must* be encompassed by the organisation's learning and development *policy*, which *should* include:

(a) ensuring that appropriate training is provided to *personnel*
(b) ensuring that all *supervisors* and managers receive appropriate training
(c) a *procedure* to evaluate training
(d) a learning and development *plan* for all *personnel*.

Departments may be subject to their organisation's policy or may have their own policy.

Effective learning and development policies can prove to be invaluable to organisations by promoting the development of members of personnel. This can support personnel retention activities as well as being a means to ensure that clients are aware of an organisation's commitment to improve the quality of its services/products.

Supervisors and managers will be required to undertake some form of supervision/management training. The type and frequency of the training will be determined by a department's needs and should align with its business strategy.

Ensuring that a department's personnel are appropriately trained will help the department to thrive. The policy should encompass the key areas that the department considers vital to its success, for example, case management. Each person within a department has a set of skills and by understanding the current level of skills and knowledge of personnel, a department can address any gaps and incorporate them into a learning and development plan, as required by 4.3(d).

4.4 The organisation or department *must* list the tasks to be undertaken by all *personnel* within the department usually in the form of a *role profile*.

A role profile details the essential and required/desired skills, knowledge, and experience necessary for a particular role or post. A job description details the tasks and responsibilities of the position. Often the role profile and job description are contained within the same document.

All personnel within a department must have a role profile or similar documentation in place. The precise format of the job documentation will be at the department's discretion, but typically it should include the job title and then cover the jobholder's place in the organisation, reporting lines, the main purpose(s) of the role and a list of specific responsibilities.

It is acceptable to have job descriptions or specifications as an alternative to role profiles, or to include the tasks to be undertaken by personnel in their contract of employment.

It is good practice to regularly review the job skills, knowledge, experience and description. Many organisations do so at the appraisal meeting of each individual member of personnel, especially as it enables a review of the role over a suitably long timescale.

> **Assessment note:** Assessors may request to see the documentation associated with any job within the department. Where this includes documents related to an individual's appraisal consent from the individual must be sought first.

4.5 The department *must* be encompassed by the organisation's *procedures* to deal effectively with recruitment selection and progression, or have *procedures* particular to the department, which *should* include:

(a) the identification of vacancies
(b) the drafting of the job documentation
(c) methods of attracting candidates
(d) clear and transparent selection
(e) storage, retention and destruction of records
(f) references and ID checking
(g) where appropriate, the checking of disciplinary records.

It is likely that a department will be bound by its organisation's recruitment, selection and progression policy. If no such policy exists then a department will be required to have its own documented policy.

Effective recruitment by the organisation/department should significantly improve the quality of the service that is provided and reduce the risks associated with recruiting. Recruitment and selection must be a transparent process, which is seen to be as objective and non-discriminatory as possible. In many organisations there will be different arrangements for the recruitment and selection of different types of personnel, such as fee earners, trainees and secretaries. Ensuring that organisations have effective recruitment procedures in place should assist them in recruiting the most suitable person for a vacancy. The procedures must include both those used internally by a department/organisation and those that are outsourced to recruitment agencies. Inclusive language must be used. The processes should be supported by having a formal and transparent process in relation to promotion and progression within a department. This may include clear role specifications for all role types and scoring candidates on essential and desirable criteria based on experience and which can be demonstrated in the application and interview process.

It is considered good practice to consider interview questions in advance of the interview and to document them. This can help to ensure that departments gather as much information as possible during the interview and reduces the likelihood of forgetting to ask relevant questions or asking inappropriate ones. Part of the interview process may include candidates being assessed in some way. The assessment could be designed to test their technical ability or personality profile.

An organisation/department should maintain records of interview notes, at the very least to assist them in defending any potential claim of unfairness in the process. An organisation/department should note that merely having notes of the interview will not in itself defend against a claim of unfair treatment or discrimination. To ensure equality in the recruitment process, an organisation/department should consider including criteria at relevant stages of the process, for example, interview criteria and interview assessment or score sheets.

The Employment Practices Data Protection Code (Part 1) provides that interview notes should not be kept for longer than one year.

Once an organisation/department has selected the candidate it would like to appoint, it must ensure that it vets the person by obtaining references, confirming his or her eligibility to work in the European Union and verifying his or her identity. In addition, it is worth considering getting proof of qualifications and P45.

The requirements in 4.5(g) encourage an organisation/department to ensure that disciplinary records of personnel are satisfactory to it. There are very few circumstances in which a department would not undertake the checks referred to at 4.5(g). The means of conducting these checks is for the organisation/department to decide. It may decide to contact the member of personnel's professional body or obtain a signed declaration from a candidate confirming his or her disciplinary record status.

Assessment note: Departments must ensure that the requirements are documented. Assessors may look for evidence of such documentation as well as any other recruitment policies within an organisation. Assessors may interview those within a department who have been involved in the recruitment process, from both employer and employee perspectives. In addition, assessors may ask to see records of any recruitment campaigns carried out, subject to confidentiality.

When assessors are seeking evidence of compliance with 4.3 they should be aware that a department may be entirely bound by its organisation's policy. In such circumstances assessors should accept the policy and should not raise a non-compliance in the event that subclauses are not adhered to, as they are not mandatory.

4.6 The department *must* be encompassed by the organisation's induction arrangements for *personnel*, or have arrangements particular to the department, including those transferring roles within the organisation and *should* cover:

(a) the management structure and the individual's responsibilities
(b) terms and conditions of employment
(c) immediate training requirements
(d) key *policies*.

Personnel joining a department may be required to attend a general induction held by the organisation or a specific induction held by the department. Typically there is a combination of both.

The induction held by a department would typically cover the following key areas:

- Information security.
- E-mail and internet access.
- Social media.
- Health and safety.
- Equality and diversity.
- Risk management policy.
- Anti-money laundering policy (if applicable).
- Anti-bribery.
- Client care.

Assessment note: There is no need to document how induction training is provided, but assessors will need sufficient evidence that the induction is effective. Assessors may ask to see any records of induction and/or interview members of personnel who have had an induction recently, to ascertain compliance.

4.7 The department or their organisations *must* have a *procedure* which details the steps to be followed when a member of *personnel* ceases to be an employee, which *should* include:

(a) the handover of work
(b) exit interviews
(c) the return of property belonging to the organisation.

The procedure referred to at 4.7(a) should include whether the person leaving needs to prepare notes for the person taking over his or her work. In addition, the procedure should state whether there is to be a handover period, during which the member of personnel who is exiting and the person taking on the role work together.

The purpose of an exit interview is to find out what a department/organisation is doing well and what it could improve upon in the opinion of employees. Below are some examples of questions that a department may wish to ask during exit interviews:

- What prompted you to seek a new job?
- Why are you leaving?
- Did you share your concerns with anyone prior to deciding to leave?
- What have you enjoyed about working here?
- What have you disliked about working here?
- How would you describe the supervision you have received?
- Did you have adequate resources to fulfil your role?
- Do you have any suggestions as to how we could be a better employer?

It is acknowledged that it is not always possible or appropriate to conduct exit interviews, for example, where a member of personnel declines to attend an exit interview or is in the process of being made redundant or being dismissed.

In addition to ensuring that the organisation's property is returned in accordance with 4.7(c), the department/organisation should consider any steps that it should take to ensure that the information management and security policy referred to at 3.1 is adhered to, for example, disabling access to the organisation's network and disabling e-mail accounts. Property that often needs to be returned includes:

- laptops;
- mobile devices;
- fob keys to access the network remotely;
- keys; and
- cars.

Departments may find it beneficial to have a set of documents including checklists and interview questions to assist with staff leaving procedures.

Assessment note: Assessors will review exit interview records, in order to ensure that a department has met this requirement. Assessors must ensure that if the records contain confidential or private information then the relevant permission has been obtained. Assessors may also seek interview evidence from those members of personnel who conduct exit interviews.

4.8 The department *must* be encompassed by the organisation's performance management *policy* or have a *policy* that is particular to the department, which *should* include:

(a) the organisation or department's approach to performance management
(b) performance review periods and timescales.

Departments will usually be subject to their organisation's performance management policy. However, if an organisation-wide policy does not exist, a department must have its own policy.

The performance management policy should include the following information:

- How performance is reviewed.
- Further development of personnel.
- Set objectives that should align with the organisation's/department's strategic plan (see 1.2).
- Available support and resources.
- Training needs.

Where personnel are involved in activities that support the organisation's equality and diversity policy, these activities should be reflected appropriately in individual performance management reviews.

The requirement in this section for written records and documented procedures is to ensure that any issues are addressed. Written records of the discussions and agreements emerging from the process are vital.

Performance reviews can take a variety of forms, for example mentoring, appraisals or score card systems. An effective performance review scheme is essential to the performance management programme of most organisations. This does not necessarily mean, however, that the same documentation should be used for all personnel or that the process should be unduly bureaucratic. Legal advisors and support staff, in particular, may be subject to quite different arrangements from each other.

It is common practice to review training needs for jobholders within the review meeting, perhaps in conjunction with other training reviews throughout the year. This information should assist with generating a training plan.

Performance review records are sensitive and will need to be subject to controls under data protection compliance considerations. A department/organisation should make clear who has access to records and for how long they are to be retained.

> **Assessment note:** Assessors may only examine personnel records with the express consent of the member of personnel in question. Records will be examined for their compliance with the organisation's/department's policy.

4.9 The department or the organisations *must* have a whistleblowing *policy*.

A department will usually be subject to its organisation's whistleblowing policy. However, if there is no organisation-wide policy, a department must have its own policy.

The whistleblowing policy should set out the types of issues that should be reported, what is unacceptable in respect thereto and to whom any such concerns should be reported. In addition, the policy should set out whether personnel should initially contact their line manager and to whom they should report the matter if it relates to their line manager.

The person that is notified of the issue should make it clear that the whistleblower can request that his or her concerns and allegations are treated in confidence and that he or she will not be penalised for taking steps to notify senior staff of his or her concerns.

The policy should make reference to key legislation such as the Public Interest Disclosure Act (PIDA) 1998 which applies to the majority of workers and employees in Great Britain. There has been subsequent legislation such as the Enterprise and Regulatory Reform Act 2013, which addresses the circumstances that give rise to criminal offences, risks to health and safety and failures of a department to meet legal obligations or miscarriages of justice and environmental damage.

It is also good practice to include information about the public interest test which was introduced by the government on 25 June 2013 and gives whistleblowers legal protection provided that certain procedures have been followed.

Assessment note: Assessors will review the policy and gather interview evidence to ensure that the policy is understood by personnel. In particular, assessors may seek to verify that personnel understand the types of behaviour that should be reported, to whom they should report and the protection offered to the person reporting.

4.10 The department or the organisations *must* have a *flexible working policy.*

Departments are usually subject to their organisation's flexible working policy due to legal obligations. However, if an organisation does not have a policy, a department must have its own policy.

Organisations/departments must take steps to ensure that the flexible working policy adheres to current legislation.

Issues that should be addressed as part of the policy include the following:

- Flexibility as to where personnel are based.
- When and at what times personnel work.
- The total number of hours that personnel work.

For example, working times, location or the pattern of work may be varied.

The flexible working policy should also set out whether the arrangements are formal or informal.

The flexible working policy should clearly set out a fair and accessible process for personnel to request an alternative working practice and how such requests are to be considered. The policy should support individuals to develop their full professional potential, regardless of working patterns.

It is good practice for the policy to define the various types of flexible working arrangements that the organisation will consider, for example, compressed hours, part-time working, job sharing, remote working or flexible start and finish times.

It is considered good practice to include in the policy flexible working request forms and impact assessment forms to be completed by personnel when requesting a flexible working arrangement.

Organisations are encouraged to be innovative and to harness technology and management skills to ensure flexible working arrangements are effective for all stakeholders, including the organisation, the department, clients and personnel.

A review of the policy must take place at least annually. Issues to be considered include changes in legislation (although this should also be considered throughout the year), whether the policy is effective, technological advancements and any lessons learned from the previous 12 months that could improve the policy.

For more information on flexible working please see the Law Society's practice note on flexible working, which can be found at **www.lawsociety.org.uk/advice/practice-notes/flexible-working**.

Assessment note: The flexible working policy may form part of the equality and diversity policy or be a standalone policy. Assessors will gather interview evidence as well and review the policy. With express permission from relevant personnel, assessors may also access records of requests for flexible working, impact assessments and any other job documentation which may contribute to the overall level of compliance of this policy.

5 RISK MANAGEMENT

5.1 The department *must* be encompassed by the organisation's risk management *policy*, or have a *policy* that is particular to the department, which *should* include:

(a) a compliance *plan*, if relevant
(b) a *risk register*
(c) defined risk management roles and responsibilities
(d) arrangements for communicating risk information.

Risk is often defined as the likelihood and impact of an event. Departments/organisations are free to define risk in the context of their working environment. The next step is to consider what a department/organisation is trying to achieve by having a risk management policy and communicate this to personnel, as personnel need to understand the behaviours required of them. The risk management policy will need to be tailored to a department's/organisation's profile and tolerance to risk. Ideally, a department/organisation should undertake an analysis of risk issues from a strategic, operation and compliance perspective.

A compliance plan should set out the ways in which a department will comply with its regulatory obligations in respect of, for example:

- the SRA;
- health and safety;
- anti-money laundering;
- anti-bribery; and
- data protection.

The risk register often divides the risks into the following categories:

- Strategic.
- Financial.
- Operational.
- Compliance.
- Breaches (material and non-material).

The register collates risks. It may be held electronically or on hard copy.

An organisation/department may set out the risk management roles and responsibilities in the risk policy or as part of the management structure that is required under 1.1(a). In the latter case it is then not necessary to repeat this information in the risk policy, unless this will benefit a department or its organisation.

Good communication of the risk policy is fundamental to its success. How effectively a department manages risk, by fostering open communication and ensuring information is shared, will be tested at its assessment.

Internal clients: If a department only advises and acts for internal clients, the risk management policy should include details of how it will manage any risks that may damage the organisation's reputation.

External clients: If a department advises and acts for external clients, the risk management policy should include details of how risks are to be managed in order to reduce the likelihood of complaints and claims being made against the organisation.

Assessment note: An assessor will review the policy and verify that the department has considered its key risks and identified the role that the risk policy plays in managing risk. Members of personnel will be interviewed to ensure that there is a consistent understanding of what is expected of them in order to manage risk within their role. An assessor will evaluate the effectiveness of communication channels by interviewing members of personnel and comparing the evidence gained against the policies that are documented.

5.2 The department *must* be encompassed by the organisation's outsourced activities *policy* or have a *policy* that is particular to the department, which *should* include:

(a) details of all outsourced activities including providers
(b) *procedures* to check the quality of outsourced work
(c) *procedures* to ensure providers have taken appropriate precautions to ensure information will be protected.

In order to comply with 5.2(a), departments may wish to keep a register of all the information on outsourced activities.

If a department is required to sign a provider's terms and conditions it should ensure that 5.2(c) is addressed in such terms and conditions or the department must require the provider, separately, to take appropriate steps to safeguard information. A department may wish to address 5.2(c) in its information management and security policy.

Assessment note: An assessor will check that the outsourced activities register is up to date when compared against file review and interview evidence. An assessor may wish to have sight of agreements to verify that confidentiality has been addressed.

5.3 There *must* be a named *supervisor* for each area of work undertaken by the department.

It is acceptable to make reference to roles rather than to name individuals, provided that those being supervised are aware of who is supervising them. This information may already be set out in the management structure required at 1.1(a).

> **Assessment note:** An assessor will expect this information to be documented in most instances. However, interview evidence to confirm that personnel know who their supervisor is will be accepted by assessors.

5.4 The department *must* have *procedures* to manage instructions which may be undertaken even though they have a higher *risk profile*, including unusual supervisory and reporting requirements or contingency planning.

The procedures must set out the types of matters that departments typically define as high risk and also have specific procedures to mitigate the risk, for example by having more frequent reviews of the matter file with a supervisor. The method by which departments manage each high risk matter is likely to vary, depending on the reasons as to why it is deemed to be high risk. This means that it is acceptable to set out specific procedures to manage risk on a case-by-case basis. This information should be apparent on the matter file to anyone who may undertake work on the file.

> **Assessment note:** An assessor will seek evidence from a variety of sources to verify that high risk matters are being managed in accordance with the procedures. For example, there may be a high risk register with supervisor review records. Alternatively, or in addition, there may be information on the matter file. An assessor should accept whatever method a department chooses to use in order to manage high risk matters, provided that they have evidence to support that the procedures are effective.

5.5 The department *should* maintain lists of work that it will and will not undertake. This information *should* be communicated to all relevant *personnel* and *should* be updated when changes occur.

It is acceptable for departments to state the areas of work that they will undertake and then to state that they do not undertake any other areas of work.

Departments should ensure that this information is communicated to relevant personnel and clients.

Internal clients: Departments that only act for internal clients may choose to have a very broad description of the work that they will undertake, as they may be obliged to accept all instructions from clients. It is acceptable for this information to be contained in the organisation's intranet.

External clients: It is acceptable to capture this information on an organisation's website, if a department has external clients.

Assessment note: Assessors will typically require a greater level of information from departments that offer legal services to external clients because there are more complex risk issues associated with such clients. Therefore, the nature of the work that is offered should be clear to all in order to manage risk effectively.

5.6 If the department acts or advises *external clients*, they *must* maintain details of the generic risks and causes of claims associated with the area(s) of work undertaken by the department. This information *must* be communicated to all relevant *personnel*.

Each area of law presents different risks, which change over time. It is often helpful to draw upon a legal advisor's experiences and perception of what can cause claims in his or her area(s) of work, when departments are formulating the list of risks. In addition, insurers can often advise departments on trends in respect of claims across different areas of law. It is good practice to review these lists on a regular basis to ensure that the information contained therein is up to date.

Assessment note: Where departments act for external clients, assessors will seek confirmation that the risks in each area of law are understood by personnel through interview evidence. This evidence should then be compared with documented lists. If departments only act for internal clients then this requirement may not be appropriate and assessors will accept that departments do not need to comply with 5.6.

5.7 The department *must* have a *procedure* to monitor key dates, or be encompassed by the organisation's *procedure*, which *must* include:

(a) the definition of key dates by work type for the department
(b) ensuring that key dates are recorded on the file and in a back-up system.

The system that departments adopt must ensure that the key dates are highly visible to the person with conduct of a matter and also to any others who may need to deal with a matter in the absence of the person with conduct.

Where a matter file is solely electronic, it may be acceptable to meet the requirements in 5.7 by having electronic alerts to help monitor key dates.

It is acceptable for the back-up system to be an electronic back-up, for example, where the case management system is backed up at the end of each day.

External clients: Missing key dates gives rise to a significant number of negligence claims each year. Therefore, great care should be taken to record and monitor key dates so that they are not missed.

Assessment note: Assessors will check key dates on matter files and how they are backed up. Interview evidence will assist assessors in understanding how they are monitored, so as not to be missed.

5.8 The department *must* be encompassed by the organisation's *policy* on the handling of conflicts, or have a *policy* that is particular to the department, which *should* include:

- **(a) the definition of conflicts**
- **(b) training for all relevant *personnel* to identify conflicts**
- **(c) steps to be followed when a conflict is identified.**

The policy should encompass client and own interest conflicts.

The policy should also emphasise that legal advisors are responsible for ensuring that there is no conflict of interest on their matters, even if certain aspects of the conflict check are performed by support personnel. Instigating and checking the results of a conflict check should always be within the remit of the legal advisor.

If support personnel assist in performing the conflicts of interests check, a department must take steps to ensure that they are trained to an appropriate level. Legal advisors should also receive appropriate training.

Legal advisors should be aware that a conflict of interest may arise at any time during the course of a matter and so they must treat the conflict check not as a one-off check that is solely undertaken at the outset of a matter, but rather as an issue to be considered as a matter progresses as well.

External clients: If a department acts for external clients there is a greater likelihood that a conflict of interest may arise between the department's clients. Therefore conflict of interest checks should be undertaken in a systematic fashion and the results recorded.

Internal clients: The most common conflict situations that departments should be aware of and be able to recognise are own interest conflict situations. The conflict of interest policy should include details of how to identify a conflict and how records are to be maintained. For example, in a personal interests register.

Assessment note: Assessors will gather evidence from matter files and interviews to verify that the policy is working effectively, particularly in relation to client conflicts. For departments that only advise internal clients, assessors will focus on own interest aspects of the policy.

5.9 The department *must* be encompassed by the organisation's *procedure* to ensure that all *personnel*, both permanent and temporary, are actively supervised, or have *procedures* that are particular to their department. Such *procedures must* include:

(a) checks on incoming and outgoing correspondence, where appropriate
(b) departmental, team and office meetings and communication structures, where appropriate
(c) reviews of matter details in order to ensure good financial controls and the appropriate allocation of workloads, where appropriate
(d) the exercise of devolved powers in publicly funded work, where appropriate
(e) the availability of a *supervisor*
(f) allocation of new work and reallocation of existing work, if necessary.

Regular supervision helps departments to control and monitor the implementation and use of their policies and procedures. When carried out effectively, this can create significant benefits ensuring that departments manage risk effectively. In addition, departments/organisations may often find that such processes can assist them in identifying areas where personnel require development (such as training) or other issues relating to personnel.

Departments should be aware that the onus is on the supervisor to be available and actively supervising personnel. This includes ensuring that those under supervision have a manageable workload and are carrying out work that is at an appropriate level commensurate with their qualification and experience.

Supervising e-mails can be challenging, particularly due to the increasing volume of electronic communication and document formats. Departments may supervise e-mails in a variety of ways. For example, an e-mail could be printed off and put in the matter file.

Departments/organisations may have a policy that defines which e-mails must be reviewed before they are sent and which are not subject to prior supervision. This latter option may be implemented by assigning risk categories to different types of e-mails.

As part of 5.9(b), departments should also consider whether it is appropriate for support personnel to attend team or departmental meetings, dependent upon how closely they work with legal advisors.

The implication of 5.9(c) is that there must be some form of financial review. This may be most effectively undertaken as part of the independent file reviews that are required by 5.11.

> **Assessment note:** Assessors will compare interview evidence against the documented procedure to verify compliance.

5.10 The department *must* have a *procedure* to ensure that all those doing legal work check their files regularly for inactivity.

There are two main methods of checking files for inactivity. If the files are in hard copy, legal advisors may conduct a 'cabinet trawl' on a regular basis. However, if there is a case management system or the ability to time record electronically, legal advisors can usually check when files were last worked on.

The focus of this requirement is for the legal advisor with conduct of a matter to check his or her files for inactivity. However, checking for inactivity can also be a useful supervision tool and supervisors may wish to review inactive file lists with legal advisors as part of supervision meetings.

It should be noted that it is acceptable for matters to be inactive if there is a valid reason for such inactivity, for example, waiting for the other side to respond within a certain time period. However, the purpose of 5.10 is to avoid inadvertently failing to progress a matter.

> **Assessment note:** Assessors will compare the documented procedure against interview evidence. In addition assessors will verify evidence of file reviews which indicate whether matters are progressed appropriately.

5.11 The department *must* have a *procedure* for regular, independent file reviews of either the management of the file or its substantive legal content, or both. In relation to file reviews, the department *must*:

(a) define and explain file selection criteria
(b) define and explain the number and frequency of reviews
(c) retain a record of the file review on the matter file and centrally
(d) ensure any corrective action, which is identified in a file review, is acted upon within 28 days and verified
(e) ensure that the designated *supervisor* reviews and monitors the data generated by file reviews
(f) conduct a review at least annually of the data generated by file reviews.

The purpose of independent file reviews is to check the quality of advice and file management. There may be some circumstances where it is not possible for the legal contents of a file to be reviewed as there is no other person within a department/organisation that has the legal knowledge to undertake such a review. However the quality of file management must always form part of a review.

The file selection criteria should set out the reasoning behind why and how files are selected for review. When defining the file selection criteria it is appropriate to consider the following:

- How to select a representative sample of the legal advisor's files.
- Whether files should be selected randomly.
- If the legal advisor is managing high risk matters, then whether those files should be reviewed more frequently.
- Whether to select files based on activity or lack of activity.
- Whether files which are at different stages of completion should be selected.

In respect of 5.11(c), the requirement is not that the full review be held on the matter file, but rather that it be apparent from the file that it has been reviewed and where the central record of such review may be found. It is increasingly common to have a central record of file reviews which is in an electronic format. This will be compliant, provided that it is apparent from the matter file that it has been subject to a file review and that the outcome of the file review can be easily traced.

There is no minimum requirement in relation to how many file reviews should be undertaken. However, departments need to ensure that they have sufficient information to identify trends when they undertake the annual review of data, required by 5.11(f).

Assessment note: Assessors will check that the file review system is working effectively by verifying that the department's procedure is being adhered to. In addition, the file reviews that assessors undertake should be compared to the results of the department/organisation file reviews in order to understand whether or not the assessors' file reviews are highlighting similar issues.

5.12 Operational risk *must* be considered and recorded in all matters before, during and after the processing of instructions. Before the matter is undertaken the legal advisor *must*:

(a) consider if a new client and/or matter is accepted by the department, in accordance with section 6.1 and 6.7 below

(b) assess the risk profile of all new instructions and notify the *supervisor*, in accordance with *procedures* under 5.4, of any unusual or high risk considerations in order that appropriate action may be taken.

During the retainer the legal advisor *must*:

(c) consider any change to the *risk profile* of the matter and report and advise on such circumstances without delay, informing the *supervisor* if appropriate
(d) inform the client in all cases where an adverse costs order is made against the organisation in relation to the matter in question.

At the end of the matter the legal advisor *must*:

(e) undertake a concluding risk assessment by considering if the client's *objectives* have been achieved
(f) notify the *supervisor* of all such circumstances in accordance with documented *procedures* in section 5.4 above.

Legal advisors should be aware of risk issues over the full duration of a matter, whether they relate to the risk of a client complaining or damage to the organisation's reputation.

The purpose of the concluding risk assessment should be to consider the following:

- Whether the client's objectives have been met.
- Whether the client is likely to complain.
- If the department acts for external clients, whether the legal advisor who is dealing with the matter is aware of any circumstances that may give rise to a negligence claim that have not already been notified to his or her supervisor.

A closing risk assessment should always be recorded on the matter file.

> **Assessment note:** Assessors will seek file evidence to verify that risk assessments are being undertaken in accordance with the department/organisation's policy.

5.13 If anti-money laundering legislation applies to the organisation, the department *must* be encompassed by the organisation's anti-money laundering *policy* or have a *policy* that is particular to the department, which *must* include:

(a) the appointment of a nominated officer usually referred to as a Money Laundering Reporting Officer (MLRO)
(b) a *procedure* for making disclosures within the organisation and by the MLRO to the authorities
(c) a *procedure* for checking the identity of the department's clients, if appropriate
(d) a *plan* for the training of *personnel*
(e) *procedures* for the proper maintenance of records.

The Law Society has produced a comprehensive practice note on anti-money laundering. For guidance on this topic please visit **www.lawsociety.org.uk/advice/practice-notes/aml**.

Assessment note: An assessor's role is not to audit departments against legislation but to assess them against their own policy. Assessors should take steps, however, to familiarise themselves with the current regulations to enable them to identify that all key issues are included in the policy. File reviews will provide evidence of compliance with the policy, for example, records of identity checks that may be retained on the matter file.

5.14 The department *must* be encompassed by the organisation's *policy* setting out the *procedures* to prevent bribery in accordance with current legislation or have a *policy* particular to the department.

Departments must ensure that the policy addresses current legal obligations. For further information, please see the Law Society's anti-bribery practice note at **www.lawsociety.org.uk/advice/practice-notes/bribery-act-2010**.

Assessment note: Assessors should be familiar with anti-bribery legislation. However, assessors are verifying that a department/organisation has implemented its policy, not assessing the department/organisation's interpretation of the legislation. Assessors may find it useful to access the gift register, if one exists.

5.15 The department *must* be included in the organisation's analysis of risk assessment data that is generated or undertake an analysis of risk data particular to their department. This *should* include:

(a) any indemnity insurance claims (where applicable)
(b) an analysis of client complaints trends
(c) data generated by file reviews
(d) any breaches that have been notified to the SRA
(e) situations where the department acted where a conflict existed (where applicable)
(f) the identification of remedial action.

The purpose of the annual review is to identify ways in which departments can improve their risk profile. Therefore, it is useful to draw together as much information as possible to enable departments to understand their current risk profile and any remedial action that may be necessary. By compiling all of the information set out in this requirement, departments should be able to identify trends across their department and be able to take appropriate steps to improve their risk profile.

Departments may also consider including client feedback in the annual analysis of risk assessment data, as this can provide additional insight into the client experience and possibly whether there are likely to be any future complaints or claims.

Assessment note: Assessors should be provided with a copy of the annual review of risk and any evidence that any remedial action has been carried out or is scheduled to take place. An organisation/department may determine the form of the review, but it must be documented.

6 CLIENT CARE

6.1 The department *must* have a *policy* for client care, which *should* include:

- **(a) how enquiries from potential clients will be dealt with**
- **(b) ensuring that before taking on a client, the department has sufficient resources and competence to deal with the matter**
- **(c) protecting client confidentiality**
- **(d) a timely response is made to telephone calls and correspondence from the client and others**
- **(e) a *procedure* for referring clients to third parties**
- **(f) the provision of *reasonable adjustments* for disabled clients.**

Departments must consider the key issues that will ensure the effective delivery of their services and record their commitment in this regard in a client care policy. It will be for each department to determine its approach to the style and format of documentation and, in particular, whether it forms part of a more general policy document or is produced separately.

The policy should include information in relation to:

- responsibility for client care;
- general approach of the department;
- actions that will be taken to test and improve client care; and
- specific behaviours expected from personnel when dealing with clients.

In relation to 6.1(f), departments must comply with their obligations to ensure reasonable adjustments are made for disabled clients and personnel. The duty to make reasonable adjustments applies to the provision of services in the same way as it applies in an employer–employee situation.

There is no set formula to determine whether an adjustment is reasonable. In the majority of cases, the provider of the services will be expected to make every effort to accommodate the needs of those with a disability.

When departments consider reasonable adjustments, they must give careful consideration as to whether a disabled client will be at a 'substantial disadvantage', if the adjustment is not made. This term is defined in the current legislation as being 'more than minor or trivial'.

In addition to this, outcome 2.3 of the SRA Code of Conduct requires departments to make adjustments for disabled clients without passing on the cost of such adjustments to the client.

In some circumstances, it may be useful to obtain advice from expert disability organisations who can assist with guidance, signposting and other forms of support.

The Law Society has produced a practice note that provides additional guidance. The practice note can be found at **www.lawsociety.org.uk/advice/practice-notes/equality-and-diversity-requirements--sra-handbook.**

Internal clients: If a department advises and acts for internal clients only, it may not need to include all the 6.1 subclauses in its client care policy. However, Lexcel can often help to improve relationships between departments, by considering how best to deal with internal clients and establishing a client care policy.

External clients: It is vital to manage client expectations and to deliver a consistent level of service. The client care policy sets boundaries for personnel to work within. If a department acts for external clients, it is strongly recommended that it complies with 6.1(a)–(f).

Assessment note: An assessor will compare the documented policy against interview evidence. An assessor may also review complaints and client feedback to verify whether the policy is operating effectively.

6.2 The department *must* communicate the following to clients in writing, unless an alternative form of communication is deemed more appropriate:

- **(a) where appropriate, establish the client's requirements and *objectives***
- **(b) provide a clear explanation of the issues involved and the options available to the client**
- **(c) explain what the legal advisor will and will not do**
- **(d) agree with the client the next steps to be taken**
- **(e) keep the client informed of progress, as agreed**
- **(f) establish in what timescale that matter will be dealt with**
- **(g) where appropriate, establish the method of funding**
- **(h) where appropriate, consider whether the intended action would be merited on a cost benefit analysis**
- **(i) agree an appropriate level of service**
- **(j) explain the department's responsibilities and the client's**
- **(k) provide the client with the name and status of the person dealing with their matter**
- **(l) where appropriate, the client is given the name and status of the person responsible for the overall supervision of their matter.**

The information required in 6.2(a)–(l) in essence forms the basis of the client care letter or terms of business. The level of information that it is appropriate to communicate to a client will depend significantly on the nature of such client.

Internal clients: Departments that act for internal clients must confirm in writing the information referred to at 6.2, unless they deem an alternative method of communication to be more appropriate. It is acceptable for some of the information to be omitted, such as 6.2(g) and/or 6.2(h), as there are circumstances where the provision of such information is not appropriate.

External clients: The information referred to at 6.2(a)–(l), in essence forms the basis of the client care letter or terms of business. The legal advisor must ensure that due regard is given to the SRA Handbook, particularly Chapter 1 of the Code of Conduct. The Law Society's practice note can be found at **www.lawsociety.org.uk/advice/practice-notes/client-care-letters**.

Assessment note: Assessors will seek evidence from the matter file that the client has been provided with all the information set out in 6.2. It is likely that if you act for external clients it will be necessary to provide a greater level of detail as compared to departments that only service internal clients. There may be circumstances where it is not appropriate to send the client correspondence setting out this information, even if you act for external clients. In such circumstances, assessors will seek evidence that the client has been provided with appropriate information and that a record is on the file by way of an attendance note.

6.3 Where appropriate, the department *should* have a service level or similar agreements with their client departments.

If it is appropriate to have a service level agreement or similar agreement, departments should ensure that it addresses the relevant issues in 6.2.

Assessment note: Assessors will request a copy of the agreement and verify that the file evidence is consistent with the agreement.

6.4 Where appropriate, the department *must* give clients the best information possible about the likely overall cost of the matter, both at the outset and when appropriate, as the matter progresses, in particular the department *should*:

(a) advise the client of the basis of the department's charging
(b) advise the client where the organisation will receive a financial benefit as a result of accepting instructions
(c) advise the client if the charging rates are to be increased

(d) advise the client of likely payments which the department or the client may need to make to others
(e) discuss with the client how they will pay
(f) advise the client that there are circumstances where the department may be entitled to exercise a lien for unpaid costs
(g) advise the client of their potential liability for any other party's costs.

The level of information and how appropriate it is for a department to comply with the subclauses above will depend on the nature of the organisation and its clients.

Internal clients: For departments that act for internal clients, the key cost issues that need to be communicated to the client departments will most likely relate to 6.4(d) and (g).

External clients: Departments that act for external clients should address all the issues referred to in 6.4.

Assessment note: Assessors will seek evidence on the matter files or as part of the agreements under 6.3 that the appropriate information is being provided to clients.

6.5 The department *must* be encompassed by the organisation's complaints handling *procedure* or have a *procedure* particular to the department, which *should* include:

(a) the definition of what the organisation regards as a complaint
(b) informing the client at the outset of the matter, that in the event of a problem they are entitled to complain
(c) the name of the person with overall responsibility for complaints
(d) providing the client with a copy of the organisation's or department's complaints *procedure*, if requested
(e) once a complaint has been made, the person complaining is informed in writing:
  (i) how the complaint will be handled; and
  (ii) in what time they will be given an initial and/or substantive response
(f) recording and reporting centrally all complaints received from clients
(g) identifying the cause of any problems of which the client has complained, offering any appropriate redress, and correcting any unsatisfactory *procedures*.

The procedure to deal with complaints will vary considerably, depending on whether or not a department acts for internal clients and how the organisation is structured.

Internal clients: The organisation will usually have a complaints handling procedure that the department will be subject to. However, if that is not the case, the department should establish its own procedure. As it is dealing with internal clients, it may be appropriate to involve the HR department, as there may be wider performance issues involved.

External clients: If departments act for external clients, the Legal Ombudsman's website contains a large amount of information that should assist departments in formulating their complaints handling procedure.

For more information, please visit **www.legalombudsman.org.uk**.

Departments/organisations should ideally review the analysis of complaints, as this will indicate the areas in which they are most at risk of receiving a complaint and where additional training or other support may be required.

Assessment note: Assessors will seek evidence of how complaints have been dealt with and verify whether the procedures have been adhered to. Assessors may wish to access the central complaints register, if one exists. For departments that act for internal clients, interview evidence or minutes of internal meetings may provide evidence of the procedures to deal with complaints.

6.6 The department *must* be encompassed by the organisation's *procedure* to monitor client satisfaction or have a *procedure* that is particular to the department.

Departments must monitor client satisfaction to understand their clients' perception of the service that is provided and to help make improvements to that service. The method of monitoring can vary; for example, face-to-face meetings may be most appropriate for internal clients, but questionnaires may be most appropriate for external clients.

Assessment note: Assessors will review any records of client feedback and encourage the department/organisation to use the information as part of its annual review of risk.

6.7 Where appropriate, the department *must* have a *procedure* to accept or decline instructions, which *should* include:

(a) how decisions are made to accept instructions from new and existing clients
(b) how decisions are made to stop acting for an existing client
(c) how decisions are made to decline instructions.

The nature of a department will play a significant role in how the procedure is set out and operates.

Internal clients: There may be little scope for declining instructions from internal clients due to the organisation's structure and purpose.

External clients: The procedure referred to at 6.7 should reflect and be consistent with the risk policy referred to at 5.1.

Assessment note: Assessors will compare the documented procedures against interview and file review information to assist in verifying whether the procedure is being adhered to.

7 FILE AND CASE MANAGEMENT

7.1 The department *must* ensure that the strategy for a matter is always apparent on the matter file and that in complex cases a project plan is developed.

The information that is recorded on the matter file as required by 6.2, 7.3 and 7.4 will usually reveal the strategy of the matter. However, if the matter is complex then a separate project plan is required. Essentially, the information held on the matter file, whether on hard copy or electronic copy, should 'tell the whole story' of the file, including the strategy.

This requirement forms part of the risk management framework within Lexcel. Fulfilling this requirement should help to ensure that if there is a complaint or potential claim, the file can easily be reviewed by someone other than the legal advisor and that such person would have a clear understanding of the strategy of the matter and whether the legal advisor has discharged his or her duty.

It is for departments to define what a complex matter/case is. However, departments often consider the following issues when deciding whether to create a complex case plan:

- Whether it is subject to High Court jurisdiction.
- The level of costs or potential costs.
- Whether it is, or is likely to be, a multi-party action.

> **Assessment note:** Assessors will seek evidence on the matter file to verify whether the strategy is apparent. If the matter is complex and there is a separate project plan, they will need to have sight of such plan.

7.2 The department *must* document *procedures* for the giving, monitoring and discharge of undertakings.

The procedures should address who within a department is permitted to give undertakings and the consequences for personnel, should they be found to be in breach of the procedures.

Departments may decide to subdivide the procedures for undertakings by department, as the type and frequency of undertakings can significantly vary by work type.

There is no requirement for a central register of undertakings, although some departments find them helpful and it is considered good practice. Departments may wish to use software, such as a case management system or spreadsheet to centralise undertaking records into a register. This may assist them in monitoring undertakings.

Assessment note: Assessors will compare the procedure against file and interview evidence. If a central register exists they will require access to it.

7.3 The department *must* be encompassed by the organisation's *procedure* or have a *procedure* particular to the department to:

(a) list open and closed matters
(b) ensure that they are able to identify and trace any documents, files, deeds, wills or any other items relating to the matter
(c) safeguard the confidentiality of matter files and all other client information
(d) ensure that the status of the matter and the action taken can be easily checked by other members of the department
(e) ensure that documents are stored on the matter file(s) in an orderly way.

Departments that have a case management system should find it relatively easy to comply with 7.3. However, those departments that do not have such a system will need to devise a method of complying with 7.3(a); for example, by managing the information on a spreadsheet or database.

As a general rule all records relating to a matter should be capable of being traced either by being on the file itself or by being referred to thereon. When a file is contained in a number of folders or lever arch files, there should be some method by which they can be shown to belong to the same matter. This could be by use of the client/matter reference number and an indication on each part, e.g. '1 of 2'; '2 of 2', etc. or 'Correspondence from 01.01.14 to 09.09.14', or by listing on a schedule, kept in a prominent part of the file. Where there are ancillary papers or other records they should be linked to the file in question by tagging or use of a client/matter numbering system.

Consideration should be given to all the circumstances where safeguarding the confidentiality of the client could be at risk (e.g. files being worked on during a train journey, files left in unattended cars, etc.). Where clients are seen in an open area, such as in an open plan office, there should be arrangements for consultations, even if very short, to be conducted out of earshot of other clients or visitors in the area. The requirements in 7.3(c) should align with the requirements in 3.1 relating to information management and security.

The state of matter files is an important consideration under this section. Showing key information on a file summary sheet or colour-coding of notes of meetings, reviews or letters to the client are helpful options.

Assessment note: Where computer case management systems are used, an assessor will need to check the protocols for the naming and storing of documents and for the making of regular back-ups. Assessors should follow audit trails to ensure that key documents can be located, when they are not stored on the matter file.

7.4 The department will have *procedures* to ensure that matters are progressed in an appropriate manner. In particular:

(a) key information *must* be recorded on the file
(b) a timely response is made to telephone calls and correspondence from the client and others
(c) where appropriate, continuing cost information is provided
(d) clients are informed in writing if the person with conduct of their matter changes, or there is a change of person to whom any problem with service may be addressed.

The requirements set out in 7.4 are closely aligned to those in section 6, which deals with client care, particularly the client care policy requirements in 6.1. Whether departments have electronic or hard copy files, they must ensure that key information is recorded on the file. Key information includes the following:

- Correspondence.
- Attendance notes.
- Records of conversations.
- Evidence.

Departments must ensure that evidence and/or documents that are not held on the matter file are clearly traceable to the matter file. For example, where evidence is stored in a strongroom or fireproof cabinet.

When deciding which information is key and should therefore be recorded on the matter file, it is considered best practice to record all telephone conversations, as it is not always obvious at the time which of these may contain key information.

7.4(b) requires departments to have procedures to ensure that clients and others are responded to in a timely manner. Therefore, departments must set out what they consider to be timely and manage client expectations accordingly.

7.4(c) requires departments to provide continuing cost information to their clients. Departments must inform clients of all costs before they are incurred or additional work is undertaken. However, if the original costs estimate or fee quoted has not changed since the start of a matter, it is not necessary to provide an update on costs. This applies to both internal and external clients as, for example, internal clients may have budget restraints.

Departments should consider setting a regular timeframe within which updates must be provided. This could be monthly or every three or six months, depending on the type of matter. Alternatively, departments may have a finance team or an accounting system that can provide alerts as a cost limit approaches, which would enable departments to notify clients promptly of any likely changes to costs.

Assessment note: Assessors will seek evidence on the matter file to verify that the procedures are being adhered to.

7.5 The department *must* be encompassed by the organisation's documented *procedure* for using barristers, expert witnesses and other external advisers who are involved in the delivery of legal services, or have a *procedure* particular to the department, which should include provision for the following:

(a) use of clear selection criteria in line with the equality and diversity *policy*
(b) where appropriate, consult with the client in relation to selection of advocate or other professional
(c) advising the clients of the name and status of the person being instructed, how long she/he might take to respond and, where disbursements are to be paid by the client, the cost involved
(d) maintenance of records on barristers and experts used, including evidence of assessment against the criteria
(e) *evaluation* of performance, for the information of other members of the department or organisation
(f) giving clear instructions
(g) checking of opinions and reports received to ensure they adequately provide the information sought (and, in litigation matters, comply with the rules of court and any court orders)
(h) payment of fees.

The selection criteria for experts and barristers must comply with the equality and diversity policy under 4.2. In addition, 7.5(b) states that where appropriate a client should be consulted on the choice. This is more likely to be appropriate in respect of internal clients, as they may well have a preference or they may wish to approve the choice of candidate.

Regardless of size, the most efficient and practical way to manage records relating to experts is by utilising a central register. This may be held in an electronic or hard copy form.

Departments may wish to include evidence of the selection criteria with the central records required by 7.5(d) or hold them separately.

It is acceptable to evaluate the performance of experts and barristers on a case-by-case basis and record this in an attendance note which is kept on the matter file. Alternatively, departments may centralise the records of performance evaluations of experts and barristers.

Assessment note: Assessors will verify that the procedure is working effectively by gathering evidence from files where an expert has been used and from interview evidence.

7.6 The department *must* have *procedures* to ensure that, at the end of the matter, the department:

- **(a) if required, reports to the client on the outcome and explains any further action that the client is required to take in the matter and what (if anything) the department will do**
- **(b) where appropriate, accounts to the client for any outstanding money**
- **(c) returns to the client any original documents or other property belonging to the client, if required**
- **(d) if appropriate, advises the client about arrangements for storage and retrieval of papers and other items retained (in so far as this has not already been dealt with, for example, in terms of business) and any charges to be made in this regard**
- **(e) advises the client whether it is appropriate to review the matter in future and, if so, when and why**
- **(f) archives and destroys files in an appropriate manner.**

This requirement assists departments in concluding matters for clients in a systematic manner, providing a framework of the key elements.

In relation to 7.6, it would be unusual for departments not to report the outcome of the matter to the client.

7.6(b) may not always be relevant, but, where it is, this should be completed promptly at the conclusion of the matter to ensure good financial management.

Departments should ensure that the requirements of 7.6(f) are consistent with their information management and security policy.

Assessment note: Assessors will select a sample of closed files to verify whether the procedures at 7.6 are being adhered to.